natalie abbott and vera

Dwell on These Things

**TRANSFORM YOUR HEART AND MIND
BY MEMORIZING GOD'S WORD**

Lifeway Press®
Brentwood, Tennessee

Published by Lifeway Press® • © 2024 Natalie Abbott and Vera Schmitz

ISBN: 978-1-4300-8529-4 • Item: 005846090
Dewey decimal classification: 227.6
Subject headings: BIBLE--MEMORIZING \ BIBLE. N.T. PHILIPPIANS--STUDY AND TEACHING / MEMORY

To order additional copies of this resource, write to Lifeway Resources Customer Service; 200 Powell Place, Suite 100; Brentwood, TN 37027-7707; order online at www.lifeway.com; fax 615.251.5933; phone toll free 800.458.2772; or email orderentry@lifeway.com.

Printed in the United States of America

Lifeway Women Bible Studies • Lifeway Resources • 200 Powell Place, Suite 100 • Brentwood, TN 37027-7707

EDITORIAL TEAM, LIFEWAY WOMEN BIBLE STUDIES

Becky Loyd
Director, Lifeway Women

Tina Boesch
Manager

Chelsea Waack
Production Leader

Mike Wakefield
Content Editor

Tessa Morrell
Production Editor

Lauren Ervin
Art Director

Sarah Hobbs
Graphic Designer

Contents

How to Use

GETTING STARTED

Welcome to *Dwell on These Things*! We're so glad you've chosen to do this study. Because we believe discipleship happens best in community, we encourage you to do this study together in a group setting. Or, if you're doing this alone, consider enlisting a friend or two to go through it at the same time. This will give you study friends to pray with and connect with over coffee or through text or email so you can chat about what you're learning.

Here's a look at what you can expect to find in this study.

OPENING SPREAD + QUICK WINS

This page provides an overview of all the elements involved in each week of study. You'll find prompts, instructions, QR codes, and a first look at the temporary tattoo design.

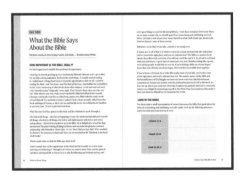

PERSONAL STUDY

Each week features five days of personal study. You'll find questions to help you understand and apply the text, plus insightful commentary to clarify your study.

TO ACCESS THE VIDEO TEACHING SESSIONS, USE THE

INSTRUCTIONS IN THE BACK OF YOUR BIBLE STUDY BOOK.

REFLECTIONS

These pages provide space for you to process and apply what you've learned during the week, plus space to interact and practice your Scripture memory with the verse designs.

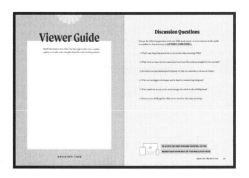

VIDEO VIEWER GUIDE & DISCUSSION QUESTIONS

On this spread, you'll be able to take notes during the video teaching and find questions to help you internalize and apply what you've heard.
These pages will drive the video teaching discussion with your group.

TEMPORARY VERSE TATTOOS

A unique resource connected to this study are temporary tattoos that help you memorize Scripture. You'll find those tattoos on a perforated card at the back of this book.

LEADING A GROUP?

A free leader guide PDF is available for download at **lifeway.com/dwell**. The leader guide offers several tips and helps along with discussion guides for each week. You'll also find free downloadable resources to help you promote the study in your church or neighborhood, including: an invitation card, promotional poster, bulletin insert, and PowerPoint® template.

Natalie Abbott

Hey, I'm Natalie. I've got five kids, and I'm married to Jason, who's a pastor. So we are full-on Jesus freaks over here! I love summer and Earl Gray tea and the Bible and fiction and poetry and pretty much all the words! I write for *Dwell Differently* and host our podcast among other things. It is seriously my dream job. I get to work with my ridiculous sister and tell people about Jesus! Who could ask for anything more?!?!

Vera Schmitz

What's up! I'm Vera, married to my college sweetheart, Matt, and mom to two boys. My favorite part of *Dwell Differently* is watching how a verse can come alive artistically, and then to see how it impacts the lives of our team, followers, and members. Thank you for letting us be a part of your walk with God—I can truly say it is one of the greatest honors of my life!

Author Letter

HEY FRIEND,

We're Natalie and Vera—sisters who love swapping clothes (yes, we still do that!), our mom's buttery homemade tortillas, and staying up way too late gabbing while we repeat for the hundredth time, "just five more minutes." We have so many shared passions, but what really binds us together is our love for Jesus and His Word. So, often you'll find us sipping tea and talking about real life—the good, the bad, and the ugly—all through the lens of our faith.

We want to invite you into that conversation in this study.

We are going to dig into Philippians 4:4-9 and study it together. And we want to help you engage both your head and your heart, letting God's truth sink in and transform you. So, we'll be memorizing and meditating on these verses right alongside you, and talking about how God is challenging, encouraging, and changing us by the power of His Word through the Holy Spirit. Our hope is that our stories will help you consider how these verses are impacting you too. Going forward, Natalie will be leading you in the written portion of the study, Vera will be showing you how to use the designs to memorize each Bible verse, and we'll both join you on the videos. We can't wait to discover the good things God has for us as we dwell on His Word together.

Thanks for joining us!

Natalie & Vera

P.S. If you want to find out more about us, you can find us on all the socials (@dwelldifferently), on our podcast (*The Dwell Differently Podcast*), or at dwelldifferently.com. We show up in those places to help people memorize one Bible verse a month—talking about what it means, why it matters, and how it's impacting our everyday lives.

Introduction

Introduction

Watch the Session One video and take notes below.

Discussion Questions

Discuss the following questions with your Bible study group. A more extensive leader guide is available for free download at **LIFEWAY.COM/DWELL**.

1. What's one thing that stood out to you in this video teaching? Why?

2. What part of Natalie's or Vera's testimony did you most resonate with and why?

3. What has been your history with memorizing Scripture?

4. What emotions are you experiencing as you begin this study?

5. What is appealing to you about this approach to Scripture memory?

6. How are you challenged by what you've heard in this video teaching?

TO ACCESS THE VIDEO TEACHING SESSIONS, USE THE

INSTRUCTIONS IN THE BACK OF YOUR BIBLE STUDY BOOK.

Why We're Here

session two

Quick Win!

This is our starting spot each week. You'll get the prompts you need to hit the ground running in knowing and memorizing each verse of Philippians 4:4-9. Today, we just want you to get familiar with the process and introduce the study. So check out the introductory video and let's get going!

Watch the short introductory video

**INTRODUCTION:
SCRIPTURE MEMORY
METHOD**

Or visit **LIFEWAY.COM/DWELL** for

all memory verse videos and Scripture art downloads.

Set Up for Success

WHY SHOULD I MEMORIZE SCRIPTURE?

That's a valid question. In a world where we have quick access to Bibles on our phones, why do we need God's Word in our heads? We can listen to the Bible and podcasts about the Bible whenever we want to. There are probably enough study guides like this one to fill up every day of the year for the rest of our lives. You can find or buy commentaries and resources to help you spend a lifetime learning about the Bible. There's even great biblical content on the internet (if you look in the right places). For most of us, God's Word is available everywhere all around us.

But access doesn't equal intimacy or application. Availability doesn't always translate to treasuring. Do you really have it with you all the time like you think you do?

Or is it just in your pocket or on your nightstand? Are you constantly dwelling on God's Word? Are His words the ones you know by heart—at the ready when you wake up with worry, or when your friend is going through something hard, or when you're scrolling through the story of your life, telling yourself who you are, what really matters, and what you're on this earth to do? Memorizing Scripture is part of what it looks like to have the Bible with you wherever you go. It means storing it in your mind and heart.

> So let me ask you, *Why do you want to memorize Scripture?* I'm not looking for the "right" answer; I'm looking for *your* answer. *Why are you here?*

Let me tell you why I am.

- I memorize Scripture because I need it. Like all the time.

- I need God's words in me speaking a better word than the words I hear from the world around me and the words I tell myself.

- I need truth to fight the lies I tend to believe.

- I need a sword to cut through the layers of my self-deception and expose the hidden sins that fester in the dark corners of my heart.

- I need the gospel of grace to pull me off the hamster wheel of trying to earn my keep with God.

- I need the security of God's love when I look in the mirror or scroll my socials.

- I need the bright light of God's Word to direct my path when I have no idea where to go.

- I need His faithful promises when my heart is heavy from praying the same prayer for years on end.

- I need a shield around me, reminding me at every blind corner that God is there with me, in control and at the ready.

- I need to hear God speaking to me in every situation and every need in real time.

- I need God's Word in me because I need God Himself!

That's why I memorize God's words, and that's why I keep on learning more and more of them. I need new words for new seasons, so that in every season I'm aware that God is walking with me and talking to me. What better thing is there?

It's the *one thing* I want to give you in this study.

This is my unswerving mission (Vera's too!)—to give everyone we can this *one thing,* the actual thing, not just a study of the thing or a book about the thing, but the thing itself: God's Word. We are desperate to give it to you. So, we've done everything we possibly can to help make memorizing Bible verses easy. We want you to walk away from this study, not just knowing *about* God's Word but actually *knowing* it, word for word. Long after this book has been recycled into paper towels and coffee filters, we hope God's words (not ours) still remain, bringing about all the good things only God can bring about in you.

YOUR THOUGHTS

Do you have a favorite Bible verse that you've memorized? What is it? Why is it your favorite?

Why do you think memorizing Bible verses is good or beneficial?

Do you experience any hesitations or hang-ups about memorizing Scripture? Why? What's one practical thing you can commit to do or practice to help you overcome those potential obstacles?

What are your hopes for this Bible study? What benefit do you hope to gain from memorizing Philippians 4:4-9?

Daily Prayer

At the end of every day of study, we will provide an interactive prayer to help you pray through what you've learned. There will be opportunities for you to thank God for what He is teaching you, confess where you are falling short, and ask for His help and direction as you seek to live out what you're learning.

O God,

Thank You for Your Word! Thank You that we can know You in it! Thank You for the truth and power and goodness in it for me. Thank You for speaking to me in Your Word. Thank You for how You've specifically used Your Word in my life in the following way:

Lord, I confess that sometimes I don't value Your Word like I should. I fill my heart and mind with other things (even good things that are not the best thing)—things that distract me or entertain me. Please forgive me for how I elevate the following things above Your Word:

Please help me value Your Word. As I memorize it in this study, please help it bear fruit in my life, so I would want to memorize it more and more.

Amen

What the Bible Says About the Bible

Fix these words of mine in your hearts and minds. — Deuteronomy 11:18a

HOW IMPORTANT IS THE BIBLE, *REALLY*?

For the longest time I couldn't have professed its importance.

I didn't go to church growing up. So, I was basically biblically illiterate until I got a Bible for my high school graduation. But here's the weird thing—I actually started reading it. I didn't know a thing about God, so I took the opportunity to find out all I could by reading the Bible. And *The Koran*. And *The Book of Mormon*. And *Siddhartha* (a Buddhist novel). And a smattering of other books about other religions. I read and read and read. I also started praying "religiously" every night, "God, if you're there, show me who you are." After about a year and a half, every book but the Bible had fallen by the wayside. I became convinced it was like no other book, maybe even filled with the actual words of God Himself. In a moment of crisis, I realized I had a choice to make: either burn that book and forget it forever or die to my sin and find life in the God of that book. Needless to say, here I am. I've yet to put that book down.

Why? Because God *has* spoken in His book, and He continues to speak through it.

The God of all things—who has no beginning or end, who made and upholds and controls all things, who knows all things, who is love and righteousness and justice and mercy and goodness—this God has spoken to us in the Bible. He is delighted to reveal the deep mysteries of His plan to bring all things in heaven and on earth into glorious, restored relationship with Himself in Christ (Eph. 1:9-11). Wow! Did you hear that? Who wouldn't be drawn to the treasures in that book? How can we not dwell on it? This book is the book of all books!

That's exactly what we find the Bible says about itself.

God is crystal clear on the significance of His Word and the benefits we receive from knowing and believing it. Through God's Word, we come to know Him and His plan of salvation and eternal life in Christ. In it we also find blessing and wisdom and joy, and every good thing we need for life and godliness. I want these treasures! Don't you? There are so many reasons why we should spend time memorizing and meditating on God's Word. Let's take a look at just a few verses that tell us what God's Word says about God's Word to discover some of those reasons.

But before we do that, let me take a minute to encourage you.

If you're new to all of this or if what you've read so far sounds awesome but also unfamiliar, you've come to the right place; you are welcome here! The Bible is a massive book about a boundless God, and none of us will ever reach the end of it. So, it's ok to not know what you don't know. I spent too many years as a new Christian feeling like a poser, worried that people would find me out. So, if you're feeling a little out of your league, know that we're all truly out of our league. We're just here to humbly learn together.

If you've been a Christian for a while (like maybe most of your life), you've also come to the right place, and you're welcome here too! The massive nature of the Bible and the boundlessness of God boggles me more and more over time. But let's be honest, sometimes we become too familiar with the profound mysteries of God in His book. So, hear me say this to you (and me!): don't take Scripture for granted! Ask God to constantly restore your delight by immersing yourself in His Word. Pray God would use this study to draw you closer to Himself as you memorize His words.

LOOK IN THE BOOK

I've chosen just a small representation of verses from across the Bible that speak about the value of memorizing and meditating on God's words. Look up the following references and write what you learn from each verse.

JOSHUA 1:7-8	
PSALM 119:11	
JOHN 20:30-31	

HEBREWS 4:12-13	
2 TIMOTHY 3:16-17	
COLOSSIANS 3:16	

Of all the benefits and promises listed in these verses, which one stood out the most to you? Why?

What are some reasons you want to memorize Scripture?

Daily Prayer

O God,

Your Word is as profound and wonderful as You are. Thank You for speaking to us through it and thank You for all the benefits we have from memorizing and meditating on its truth. Thank You especially for this:

Lord, I want to live out Your words as the foundation for my life, but so often I don't. Forgive me for not valuing Scripture, especially when it comes to this part of my life:

God, please help me to elevate my view of Scripture. Please help me grow in my practice of spending time in it regularly in this way:

I praise You for all the good things You have for me in Your Word. Thank You for forgiving me when I fall short. And thank You for helping me by the power of Your Spirit to understand and desire Your Word more and more.

Amen

Dwell on These Things

Finally, brothers and sisters, whatever is true, whatever is noble, whatever is right, whatever is pure, whatever is lovely, whatever is admirable—if anything is excellent or praiseworthy—think about such things. — Philippians 4:8

WHAT ARE YOU DWELLING ON?

Before we start memorizing and meditating on the good and true words of God, it's important to take an inventory of what we're tempted to and tend to dwell on instead.

> So, what have you been dwelling on in the past week or so? What did you put in your heart and mind? What did you read, watch, or listen to? What messages did you hear about what's true, what matters, who you are, what you were made for, and what's happening in the world?

I'm sure you listed a whole range of things from substantiated facts to harmless nothingness to advertising schemes to shameful junk to absolute lies. It's probably a lot to sort through. Our lists show the many messages we hear and see on any given day. And oftentimes, we can be unintentional with so much of our thought lives.

We should be more intentional.

Paul, in his letter to the Philippians, gave us an extensive list of what we should be putting in our minds.

> *Finally, brothers and sisters, whatever is true, whatever is noble, whatever is right, whatever is pure, whatever is lovely, whatever is admirable—if anything is excellent or praiseworthy—think about such things.*

> PHILIPPIANS 4:8

See what I mean? That's pretty exhaustive. I can't think of any good thing that falls outside that list. Can you imagine your mind being filled with things like this all the time? We can and should be intentionally directing and redirecting our minds to dwell on such things. Tomorrow we'll see how Scripture is the fulfillment and culmination of every good thing we should dwell on.

Not just some of the time but all the time.

Paul gave us a comprehensive list of things to think on and told us to think on them constantly. The constant part isn't apparent in most English translations, but in the original language (Greek) it's very clear. The Greek word for *think* is a present middle imperative verb, which indicates a command that is to be continuously obeyed.[1] The Amplified Bible translation reflects this meaning: "think continually on these things." In other words, we're never not supposed to have our heads filled with such thoughts. The CSB translation says we are to, "dwell on these things." I love this translation because the word *dwell* carries this nuance of deeply and constantly meditating on something. This is one of the main reasons we titled our study *Dwell on These Things*, because that is what we are going to do. We aren't just going to learn about the value of dwelling on these things; we're going to do so by memorizing and meditating on six Bible verses.

HOW IT WORKS

Vera and I have been helping people memorize Scripture for many years through our company, Dwell Differently. We use a simple, proven method that works.

1. We start with a verse.

Finally, brothers and sisters, whatever is true, whatever is noble, whatever is right, whatever is pure, whatever is lovely, whatever is admirable—if anything is excellent or praiseworthy—think about such things.

PHILIPPIANS 4:8

2. We take the first letter of each word in the verse and string them together in a long line of letters.

F B A S W I T W I N W I R W I P W I L W I A I A I E O P T A S T

3. We take the letters and turn them into a beautiful Scripture design.

4. Every time you see the design image, you're challenged to recall what each letter represents. Eventually, you memorize the verse.

It really is that simple. The image is intentionally designed to help you recall not just the verse itself but also the message of the verse. Since this verse is about dwelling on the true and lovely things of God, we chose the image of a flower. We've included temporary verse tattoos of each design for you to use as reminders. (You'll find them on the perforated card at the back of this book.) Place the temporary verse tattoo somewhere you'll see it often, such as on your wrist. Then, when you see it throughout your day, it will help you recall the verse and its meaning.

For now, imagine how different your life might look if you already had this verse in your head urging you to constantly think about all the good things listed. Let's consider how you might apply Philippians 4:8. Choose a few of the following questions to answer.

How can keeping in mind what is true help when you're struggling to refute a lie about who you are in Christ or what you're called to do?

How can dwelling on what is noble keep you from entertaining dishonorable thoughts about someone?

How can constantly considering what is right help you make tough decisions?

How can reminding yourself you are pure in Christ help you when you struggle with shame over sin?

How can thinking on what God says is lovely help you filter the mixed-bag messages of the world?

How can constantly considering what is admirable help you live a life worthy of respect?

How can dwelling on morally excellent things help you with holy living?

How can filling your mind with praiseworthy things prompt you to praise God, who is the Source of those things?

How is Jesus the fulfillment of each of these virtues?

This is just a taste of where we're headed! We won't actually focus on this verse until Session Seven, but the message in it is foundational for the study itself. I can't wait for us to build on it in the coming weeks.

Daily Prayer

Dear Lord,

Thank You for all the good things we can know about You in Your Word. Thank You that Scripture is filled with all that is true, noble, right, pure, lovely, admirable, excellent, and praiseworthy. Specifically, thank You for this particular good thing I know from Your Word:

Lord, as I think about the list in Philippians 4:8, I am at a loss. Too often, I don't fill my mind with those things. Instead, my mind is filled with the following specific things that draw my attention away from You:

Forgive me and help me change what I dwell on.

Lord, You are a God who is full of truth and grace. Please pour out Your grace on me as You pour out Your truth in Your Word.

Amen

Finding Meaning in Philippians

DON'T SKIM THIS!

I have a confession.

I'm actually kind of embarrassed to say it, but here goes. I was an English major in college, but I didn't read all my assignments.

I hear my professors whispering, "For shame."

I mean, I had good reasons. It was a lot of reading, and some of it was particularly boring (at least to me). I can't tell you how many times I fell asleep trying to read *Beowulf*. I finally gave up. I did skim it, but if you've ever read Old English, you know that was a huge fail, and my quiz grade reflected it. Even though I read parts of it, I really had no earthly idea what was going on in that epic poem. I still don't. The point: it was silly of me to think I could skim that poem and understand it. That assessment probably holds true for any book of substance.

Yet, most of us do this very thing with the Bible all the time.

Often, we treat the Bible more like a search engine than the story of God. We go to it looking for help with our marriages or how to raise a difficult child. We search through it looking for guidance in a big decision. We dig through it looking for words to comfort our broken hearts. This isn't wrong. The Bible does speak to those issues, and there is so much wisdom in it for us. But if picking out parts is all we're doing, we're missing so much! More than that, we run the risk of misunderstanding the bigger story.

We aren't going to do that here.

Instead, in this study, we're going to read, study, and memorize our verses in the context of the whole book. Not the whole Bible (that'd take way too long!), but the whole book of Philippians. It's four chapters long and should only take about twelve to fifteen minutes to read. Getting this broader context is so important for understanding what our focus verses are saying. Going forward, we'll be referencing parts of the letter again and again. Why? Because everything Paul said in our six memory verses is also mentioned in other parts of the letter, sometimes repeatedly.

Think about it this way: the whole book of Philippians is the lens through which we can and will most clearly see our memory verses. So today, we're going to read through Philippians and answer some questions to establish and understand context.

LOOK IN THE BOOK

Read through Philippians and answer these questions.

What are some of the things you can gather about the author? Where was he writing from? What was he concerned or excited about? Who was with him?

What can you tell about the recipients of this letter? What might have been some of their struggles and triumphs?

How did Paul feel about the Philippians? How did he communicate and express those feelings?

What are some of the themes or important ideas that you notice? What are repeated words or phrases?

What stands out to you or makes you pause?

What questions do you have?

Hopefully, you were able to get a good sense of Paul's love for this church and what he wanted to communicate to them. This will set us up well for next week when we start studying our verses one at a time.

Daily Prayer

Dear Lord,

Thank You for the book of Philippians. Thank You for its goodness and beauty. Specifically, thank You for this part:

Forgive me when I come to Your book just looking for a quick answer, not really looking to meet You. I think of the recent time this happened:

Lord, please give me all the things I need to do this study—the time, the patience, the space, the wisdom, and the commitment. I especially need Your help with:

I praise You, God, that You have me in this passage of Scripture in this season of my life. I trust that You will use it for my good and Your glory!

Amen

God's Word Applied

In each session of this study, Day Five is your reflection day. We'll give you space and time to process all the things you've learned throughout the week. There's a lot of blank space here. Don't be intimidated by it. You don't have to fill it up. Use it to journal notes, quotes, and things to remember. Record your thoughts and prayers as you seek God and find what He wants you to know, understand, and live out.

I've listed some questions to help you get rolling, but don't feel like you need to answer all (or any) of them.

- What are the most significant things you learned this week? What were your "aha moments," if any?

- Write out a favorite verse you've memorized (or want to memorize) and tell why.

- Is there a particular verse God is using in your life in this season? What is it and why?

- Of the list of virtues from Philippians 4:8, which one do you most want to live out? Why?

- What was the most interesting thing you learned from reading through Philippians?

Reflections

Reflections

Dwell on These Things

Daily Prayer

Write your own prayer today. Thank God for specific things you appreciate about His Word. Confess your lack of valuing God's Word like you should. Ask God to continue molding you into someone who loves His Word more and more and whose life reflects that love.

_____

_____

_____

_____

_____

_____

_____

_____

_____

_____

_____

_____

_____

_____

_____

_____

_____

_____

Viewer Guide

Watch the Session Two video. Use this page to take notes, capture quotes, or doodle some thoughts from the video teaching session.

Discussion Questions

Discuss the following questions with your Bible study group. A more extensive leader guide is available for free download at **LIFEWAY.COM/DWELL**.

1. What's one thing that stood out to you in this video teaching? Why?

2. What verse or verses you've memorized have been the most meaningful to you and why?

3. How has God used memorized Scripture to help you minister or witness to others?

4. What are the biggest challenges you've faced in memorizing Scripture?

5. What stood out to you as you read through the whole book of Philippians?

6. How are you challenged by what you've heard in this video teaching?

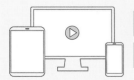

TO ACCESS THE VIDEO TEACHING SESSIONS, USE THE

INSTRUCTIONS IN THE BACK OF YOUR BIBLE STUDY BOOK.

Searching for Joy

Quick Wins!

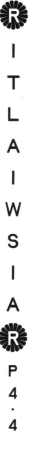

- Download the Scripture art to your phone, watch, or computer

- Watch the short memory verse video

- Apply the temporary verse tattoo found at the back of your Bible study book

SCRIPTURE ART DOWNLOAD

MEMORY VERSE: PHILIPPIANS 4:4

Or visit **LIFEWAY.COM/DWELL** for all memory verse videos and Scripture art downloads.

Set Up for Success

Rejoice in the Lord always. I will say it again: Rejoice!
— Philippians 4:4

YOUR FIRST THOUGHTS

Before we start studying Philippians 4:4, let's take a first glance and see what we see.

What does this verse tell us about God?

What's your initial response to this verse? What does it make you think about? What emotions do you experience when you read the verse and why?

Does it bother you that Paul commanded you to rejoice? Why or why not? Why might you need to hear this command?

What do you think rejoicing *in the Lord* means? How might that phrase color our understanding of this command?

Paul told his readers to rejoice in the Lord *always*. When is rejoicing easy for you? When is rejoicing hard?

Have there been times you were able to rejoice even when you didn't feel like it? If so, how were you able to do so? If not, why did you struggle?

Where are you at this moment with this command to rejoice in the Lord always?

We're on the hunt for joy this week, but not just any joy—joy *in the Lord*. Where can we find joy like that? Joy that isn't dependent on our circumstances. Joy when we don't feel joyful. Joy when it feels scarce and precious.

MY THOUGHTS

Personally, I've been on the lookout for joy all week.

My oldest son left for college a few short days ago, and I feel his absence deeply—after school, at our table, at church. He's not here. He's off living his life, following his next step. This move is right and good. He's so completely ready. In my mind I know I should be rejoicing. But this momma's heart is struggling to do so. It's like a part of me moved away when he did. And I'm having trouble finding joy.

It feels ironic, maybe even a bit hypocritical, to encourage you to rejoice when rejoicing is the very thing I'm struggling to do. But maybe, just maybe, God, in His mercy, has me in the thick of this struggle right now because you might also be in the thick of a similar one. Maybe you're having trouble rejoicing in some circumstance—a diagnosis, a difficulty, a relationship. Maybe this is a raw place for you. I pray I can walk tenderly with you through this verse, knowing joy can feel elusive at times. That's how it feels for me right now.

Like I mentioned earlier, I agree with the verse in my mind (I have so many reasons to rejoice in the Lord!), yet in my heart, I feel affronted. I'm knocked down. Can I make myself rejoice? Can I say this verse with any real honesty? At first read it bothers me that Paul commanded rejoicing. It feels like he shouldn't. It feels like Paul is following me around as I recite this verse, poking his bony finger straight at my heart, telling me to do the very thing I can't find in myself to do: Rejoice. And he's relentless. He repeats it: *Rejoice!*

What's an honest person to do? Fake it 'til I make it?

Let me be clear: I want that joy. Like really, *really*! I'm not over here shaking my head with my heels dug in saying, "No way am I going to rejoice!" Quite the opposite. I *want* deep joy in my heart. I'm not sure how to get there, but I'm willing to try!

So, here's the first thing I'm doing: being honest with God about this struggle.

For the past couple of mornings, I've been getting up and fighting for joy with God's truth. Here's my approach:

1. **I confess my inability and even unwillingness to rejoice.**

2. **I ask God to help me find my joy in Him.**

3. **I preach this verse to myself. Like all day long. When the waves and breakers of sadness roll over me, when someone asks if I miss Josiah or how I'm holding up, when my hurting heart swells to burst, I speak these words to my soul: "*Rejoice in the Lord*, always!" *What's that? Having trouble?* "I will say it again: REJOICE!"**

That's it. And here's the thing—it is helping. Significantly.

Why? God is always faithful to meet me in His Word. They are His words. True words. Words I need when things are hard, when I'm not feeling joy, when I feel anxious about my circumstances, or I just need direction. This is why I keep on memorizing His words. They are His words for me. Right now and always. I hope that as you memorize them, they would become His words for you also.

So, here's my ask: Whether you're feeling completely empty or your heart is already full of joy, will you join me in the search for joy? Let's look for why Paul was so joyful in his letter. Let's discover the reason for Paul's audacity to command joy in others. Step out with me and discover God's heart for us in this verse. I'm convinced that as we start to understand the answers to these (and more) questions as we meditate on this verse this week, we may just move our joy meter in the right direction. I want that! Do you?

Daily Prayer

Here's a reminder: all the daily prayers are interactive. The one below is similar to the prayer I've been praying each morning for the past few days. Use it as a guide to close your study. Afterward, spend some time reciting and meditating on the verse.

O God,

I know in my mind that You have given me so many reasons to rejoice in You. Yet, there are parts of my heart that just aren't joyful. They are weighed down with hard things. Lord, I confess that I have trouble rejoicing because of these specific things:

Conversely, here are some things I'm rejoicing in more than or even instead of You:

I repent of this and ask for Your forgiveness. I long to rejoice in You, not merely in your blessings!

I long to rejoice in You, my God, and to overflow with deep joy that comes from You. Here are some of the reasons I will rejoice in You today:

I say to my soul, "Rejoice in the Lord always. I will say it again: Rejoice!" As I learn and repeat these words, make them come alive to me. Spirit, open my eyes to see all You have to teach me. Renew my mind with Your truth. Change my heart to one that overflows with contagious joy. I praise and thank You that this is Your heart for me and You will aid me in this journey.

Amen

Reasons for Rejoicing

Rejoice in the Lord always. I will say it again: Rejoice! — Philippians 4:4

THIS IS *MY* JOY!

So far, we've just scratched the surface of our verse for this session. Here's what I hope is happening:

- The introductory video and Day One reflection questions piqued your interest and left you wanting more answers.

- You're starting to memorize verse 4 as you see the Scripture art on your phone or see your temporary tattoo.

- When you read the verse just now, the words sounded familiar, and you have a longing to understand them more fully.

I'm so excited for today; you might even say I'm rejoicing! Why? Because today we start studying the Bible one tiny verse at a time—phrase by phrase, word by word. This is the point we dig in and find some answers, discover new insights, consider the nuances, and start considering how this verse might become alive and start working real heart change in us! Are you catching my excitement and joy? I hope so!

Let me give you a peak behind the curtain.

I already mentioned that I was an English major in college. The most important, lasting thing I discovered in that major (other than my deep love for every Jane Austen novel) was how to analyze a text. We're going to use that skill in this study. First, we'll identify some focus points in our verse. Then, we'll widen our lens by looking at other places in Philippians where these focus points show up. Doing so will illuminate the verse and deepen our understanding of what Paul meant when he told us to "Rejoice!" When we see this fuller picture, we'll better understand Paul's original intent and more clearly see what the verse teaches us about God, ourselves, and why it matters in our everyday lives. So, my friend, let's get digging!

WHAT'S THE POINT?

Rejoice in the Lord always. I will say it again: Rejoice!

PHILIPPIANS 4:4

I identified three focus points for us to explore:

- Rejoicing or joy

- Rejoicing *in the Lord*

- Rejoicing *always*

Next, let's format a question from each of these points to guide our search for meaning. There are different questions we could ask, but let's examine these three:

- What reasons did Paul have for rejoicing?

- What did Paul mean by the phrase "rejoice in the Lord"?

- How can we rejoice at all times?

These questions are more than we can cover today. So, we're going to tackle them over the next couple of days, starting with the first one.

LOOK IN THE BOOK

The Focus: Rejoicing or joy

The Question: What reasons did Paul have for rejoicing?

To answer our question (and discover more about joy in the process), we're going to review the whole book of Philippians again but through the lens of that question. Since you've already read the book once, I'm going to give you two routes to choose between for your approach: the long way and the shortcut. If you pick the shortcut, no judgment here, but do go ahead and read through the instructions on taking the long way. You can then put that Bible study method in your back pocket for later.

The Long Way

Read the complete letter to the Philippians. Highlight all the references and reasons Paul gave for rejoicing, or list them in a journal or separate sheet of paper. Look for the words *rejoice*, *joy*, and *glad*.

The Shortcut

Look up each of the following verses and highlight them in the same color. Write what you learn about Paul and his friends' reasons for rejoicing.

PHILIPPIANS 1:3-5	
PHILIPPIANS 1:18-19	
PHILIPPIANS 1:23-26	
PHILIPPIANS 2:1-2	
PHILIPPIANS 2:16-18	
PHILIPPIANS 3:1	
PHILIPPIANS 4:1	
PHILIPPIANS 4:4	
PHILIPPIANS 4:10	

That's a lot of rejoicing for four short chapters! When I read the verse we're currently memorizing, for some reason I'm tempted to think rejoicing must not be as important as the other concepts in our passage—like prayer and peace and having a strong mind. But it seems that rejoicing is a major theme in Paul's life and in this letter.

How might rejoicing be essential, even central to the Christian life?

Paul's joy expressed in this letter seems to fall into two main categories. Paul is either rejoicing "in the Lord" (and things pertaining to the Lord), or he's rejoicing in his friends (and things pertaining to them). We are going to tackle Paul's rejoicing "in the Lord" on Day Three. So, for now, let's consider his reasons for rejoicing in God's people.

> **Review the previous list of verses. What reasons did Paul give for rejoicing in the Philippian believers?**

> **Do you have these kinds of relationships in your church? If so, describe them. If not, why not?**

Paul loved his friends, and they brought him so much joy. But we all know that relationships in the church aren't always rainbows and puppy dogs. The same was true for the Philippian church.

Read Philippians 4:1-4.

In verses 2-3, Paul was pleading with two fellow believers (whose names are written in the book of life!) to get along. These were fellow ministry leaders who were having a major squabble. And then right afterward, he said, "Rejoice in the Lord!"

> **What does this situation teach us about reconciliation and rejoicing?**

If we have been reconciled to God through Christ, how can we hold a grudge against another person who is also reconciled to the Lord? If we want to truly and fully rejoice in the Lord, we must be reconciled to His people, forgiving them as He forgives us (Col. 3:13). Sounds easy enough, but application can be difficult. Let me poke at you a bit with my next questions.

> **Where are you struggling in a relationship with another believer? What reasons do you have to forgive, find unity, and even rejoice in that relationship? What can you do, even today, to work toward reconciliation?**

Daily Prayer

O God!

Thank You for Your Word! Thank You for Paul's example of joy in Philippians 4:4 and in the whole letter he wrote to his friends. Thank You for all the believers in my life. I thank You specifically for these friends in the faith You have given me:

I confess, some of my relationships are messy though. Lord, would You please convict my heart and bring to mind any relationship that needs to be reconciled and restored? Help me forgive, find common ground, and find reasons for rejoicing in my relationship with this person:

Oh Lord, I long to be more like Paul. I long to know and love people who I can partner with in life and in gospel ministry. Please open my eyes and heart to the people You would have me join in Your good work.

I praise You, my God! I rejoice in Your grace toward me as I learn and lean into this verse—Your words for me.

Amen

The Source of Our Joy

Fill in the blanks:

Rejoice _____ _____ _____ always.
I _____ _____ _____ _____: Rejoice!

Philippians 4:4

REJOICE *IN THE LORD*?

Last time, we noted the instances of rejoicing in Paul's letter to his friends. We found that much of his rejoicing had to do with them. He rejoiced that they shared his love for the gospel, that they supported his ministry, that they were unified, and that their faith was genuine. Today, we're going to examine the verses that talk about Paul's other reason for rejoicing—his God.

LOOK IN THE BOOK

The Focus: Rejoicing *in the Lord*

The Question: What did Paul mean by the phrase "rejoice in the Lord"?

Paul repeated the phrase "rejoice in the Lord" three different times in the letter to the Philippians (3:1; 4:4,10). Today, let's take a closer look at the context of those verses to give us more insight into what Paul meant by this command.

Read Philippians 3:1-14.

Notice that Paul started off this section by telling his friends to rejoice *in the Lord as a safeguard for* them.

> **What did Paul call the false teachers he was wanting to safeguard the Philippians from?**

Paul used strong language to warn the church about the Jewish false teachers among them. These opponents were distorting the gospel by insisting that true believers in Christ had to follow Jewish law, such as circumcision.

Paul implied that the false teachers were putting confidence in the flesh. What reasons did Paul say he too could have that kind of confidence (vv. 4-6)?

But where was Paul's confidence placed? Whose righteousness was Paul depending on?

Did you get the connection between rejoicing and safety? Paul told his friends to rejoice "in the Lord" as a safeguard for their faith because their salvation is *in the Lord*. Righteousness doesn't come from good deeds or a religious pedigree. In fact, Paul said,

I consider them garbage, that I may gain Christ and be found in him, not having a righteousness of my own that comes from the law, but that which is through faith in Christ—the righteousness that comes from God on the basis of faith.

PHILIPPIANS 3:8b-9

The reason for Paul's confidence *and* his rejoicing was that Jesus Himself had given Paul His righteousness. So, when Paul said, "Rejoice in the Lord," he wasn't just talking about the Lord as the object of rejoicing but also the Source of salvation.

In light of this understanding, how might rejoicing in the Lord (because of His salvation) prove to be a safeguard against the false teaching of works-based righteousness?

I love the idea of rejoicing in the God of our salvation as a safety measure, don't you? Rejoicing as a protective measure might seem a little strange at first. But when we understand what Paul was saying, it makes total sense! So, lean in and let me ask you a more personal question.

Are you safe?

Are you rejoicing in the Lord (in the fullest sense)? Is your spiritual confidence in Christ's saving work and His righteousness? Or are you trying to earn God's favor (and your salvation) by doing good things?

HOW TO START REJOICING IN THE LORD

Maybe this idea of rejoicing in the Lord because of His salvation is all new to you. Maybe, up until now, you would've said your salvation depends on doing enough good things to earn God's favor. If so, you are welcome here.

I used to be just like you, trying to be good enough for God. In fact, when I first heard this message of salvation through faith, I thought it was too wonderful to be true. I struggled to believe that Jesus (God's own perfect Son) would give His life as a payment for all my sins. I also struggled to comprehend that with my honest confession of not being good enough to earn my way, He would make me His own beloved daughter right now and for all eternity.

How could this be true? Why would anyone do that for me?

Because of love.

In 1 John 4:9, John wrote, "This is how God showed his love among us: He sent his one and only Son into the world that we might live through him." This is the safe salvation Paul was talking about in Philippians 3:1-14—a salvation based on the good work of Jesus on our behalf.

Do you believe that truth? Do you want to?

If so, tell Jesus. Confess your sin and believe that Jesus's perfect life, atoning death, and bodily resurrection can make you right before God. He has done and been and earned everything perfectly on your behalf. This, my friend, is the wonder of our faith and the reason for our rejoicing—Jesus loves us and has made us His own. (For more information on how to become a Christian, see page 188.)

Read Philippians 4:4-9 to see our memory verse in its immediate context. These verses are filled with commands.

Summarize what Paul directed his friends to do.

Paul encouraged them to live out their faith, and he started his list with "Rejoice in the Lord." From what we learned in 3:1-14, this statement seems to be Paul's shorthand way of encouraging them to rejoice not only in Jesus as their Lord, but in His saving work.

How might rejoicing in the Lord's salvation be a good place to start when we think about our Christian living?

Christian living can become drudgery when our lives aren't rooted in the joy we have in the Lord that comes from our salvation.

Read Philippians 4:10-13, focusing on verse 10.

Paul was rejoicing in the Lord for having his material needs met. But he went on to say he would've been content regardless because he'd learned the secret to contentment.

What was Paul's secret to contentment (vv. 12-13)?

What relationship is there between rejoicing in our spiritual salvation and having contentment regarding our physical needs?

How can you find contentment and even rejoice despite having unmet physical need?

Again and again, we see that rejoicing in the Lord and His salvation finds its good application in our lives. To rejoice in the Lord is to guard against relying on our good deeds to save us. To rejoice in the Lord is to be motivated to live our lives in ways that please Him. To rejoice in the Lord is to be content knowing our spiritual needs are met even when our physical needs aren't. So, let's rejoice in the Lord, who is both the object and the source of our joy!

Daily Prayer

O God,

I have so many reasons for rejoicing in who You are and what You have done for everyone who believes in Jesus. Thank You for Your Word that tells me to rejoice in You as a safeguard against trusting in my good deeds to save me. And yet, so often I put my confidence in my efforts as a means of earning Your favor. Lord, please forgive me for putting my confidence in the following self-efforts instead of You:

Help me instead to rejoice in You and in Your salvation. Help me wonder at Your goodness and love toward me. I thank You specifically for this part of my salvation story:

I will rejoice in You and in Your salvation today. And may my rejoicing be contagious to those around me.

Amen

R
I
T
L
A
I
W
S
I
A
R
P
4
.
4

Unceasing Joy

Write Philippians 4:4.

COMMANDING CONSTANT JOY

"Attitude is everything."

I say this all the time to my kids. I'm sure my constant use of this phrase will one day be a part of our family lore—just like my siblings and I still tease our mom for her catch phrases: "drink from the hose" and "I can't do all the things for all the people all the time" and "I'm going to throw all your stuff in the biggest box in the nation." I laugh out loud just saying those here. But I just realized something about my repetitive phrase concerning attitude.

I am a hypocrite.

Here I am, all offended that Paul would have the audacity to command constant joy, and yet I am doing the exact same thing. Day in and day out, I'm telling my kids that "attitude is everything," with the implication being: change your attitude. Adopt what kind of attitude? You guessed it! Joy! Here's what I'm thinking: *Even if your hands are doing the right thing, but you've got a chip on your shoulder and your heart is far, far away, I want your attitude to change. Be joyful, like all the time.*

I bring this up not only to clear my conscience, but because this constant command for joy is what we're talking about today. Paul told his friends to "Rejoice in the Lord always." How do we even do that? How do we muster up joy when rejoicing is difficult or when we just aren't feeling it? Do we have to fake it? Or is obedience to this command actually possible?

You know where we are headed for these answers: back to the Book!

LOOK IN THE BOOK

The Focus: Rejoice *always.*

The Question: How can we rejoice at all times?

Read Philippians 1:12-26.

In this section of Scripture Paul made three references to joy despite multiple reasons to not be joyful. (If you don't already have the references to joy highlighted in verses 18 and 25, go ahead and highlight them now.)

What difficult situation was Paul facing (vv. 12-14)?

For what reason could Paul rejoice despite the difficulty (v. 14)?

What problem did Paul mention in verses 15-18?

Why was Paul so unconcerned with his rivals? What was the source of his ability to rejoice?

What reasons did Paul give for rejoicing in verses 18-19?

What did Paul mean by "For to me, to live is Christ and to die is gain"?

In the midst of his struggle of not knowing whether he would live or die, Paul told his friends he had reason to rejoice. Why? His joy was in Jesus and making Him known. Whether Paul's rivals were preaching Jesus from pure motivations or not, Jesus was preached, and that result gave him joy. Whether Paul was in prison or not, he was preaching Jesus, and that reality gave him joy. Even if he died, Paul knew he would be with Jesus and his joy would be fully realized.

Paul was committed to sharing his Jesus-fueled joy. Notice verses 25-26. Paul welcomed and longed for the in-person glorious joy of heaven but was willing to wait in order to encourage the spiritual progress and joy of his friends!

What challenges you about Paul's commitment to his friends' spiritual growth and joy?

What is one practical way you could be more committed to the spiritual growth and joy of the people (or just one person) in your life?

What are some things that make it hard for you to find joy?

How does Paul's example of rejoicing in every circumstance motivate your own ability to rejoice in suffering?

Paul was rooting for the day when he got to "depart and be with Christ." He knew that destination was far better than sticking around on earth. Why? Because Jesus was the source and the object of his joy. He rejoiced *in the Lord*. And he longed for the culmination of this wondrous joy: face-to-face with Jesus for eternity. Jesus—who lived and died and rose again on his behalf. Jesus—whose righteousness he now had. Jesus—whose salvation was safe. This was the Jesus who loved Paul and who he longed for. Jesus was the reason for Paul's joy. Yet, he would remain, not for his own joy but for the joy of his friends and their continued progress in the faith.

Paul's joy depended on Jesus, whether he was in prison or out, whether his opponents preached from false motives or true, whether he was alive or dead. Jesus was always Jesus. And therefore, Paul's joy in Jesus was an "always" kind of joy.

This "always" kind of joy is possible for us too! We can have joy in every circumstance when our joy is rooted in Jesus. And whenever we forget this truth, may the words of verse 4 be the reminder to our souls that we can indeed, "Rejoice in the Lord *always*!"

Daily Prayer

O God,

Thank You for Paul's example of joy in all circumstances. I confess I sometimes feel overwhelmed and find it difficult to rejoice always. Please help me find my joy in You, even in these difficult circumstances:

Lord, I long to be more like Paul in my love for You. I long to say as he said: to live is Christ and to die is gain. Jesus, here are some of the reasons I find my joy in You:

I praise You that You love me and I have joy in You. Thank You that my joy doesn't depend on my ever-changing circumstances. Rather my joy is secure in You. I will rejoice in You always!

Amen

Joy Applied

Have you memorized Philippians 4:4 yet? Write it out here.

R
I
T
L
A
I
W
S
I
A
R
P
4
.
4

What a powerful verse! I'm grateful for what we have learned about it. But what good is knowing a verse and its implications if we never let it change our hearts? So today we're going to spend time meditating on what we've learned and asking God to show us where we can start practically living this truth. We've provided reflection prompts and space for you to respond. But don't feel like you have to use all the prompts and fill up all the space. It's here if you need it. May the Lord meet you here and bless you in this time!

- What are the most significant things you learned? What were your "aha moments," if any?

- Where did the Holy Spirit convict you while studying this verse?

- What changes do you need to make in your thoughts, attitudes, or actions?

- How did your perspective of this verse change through the week as you studied it and meditated on it?

- Would you say you have Christian friendships like Paul had? If so, what can you do to maintain and strengthen them? If not, how can you foster these kinds of friendships?

- Write out a list of all the reasons you have for rejoicing!

Reflections

Verses

FBAS

WIT
WIN
WIR

WIP
WIL
WIA

IAIEOPTAST
P4.8

WYHLOR
OHFM
SIM
PIIPAT
GOPW
BWY P4.9

ug
bet
atL
in
p4.
5

DNBAAABIES
BPAPWT

PYRTG

P4.6

ATPOG WTAU WGYH AYM ICJ P4.7

R
I
T
L
A
I
W
S
I
A
R
P
4
·
4

Daily Prayer

Write your own prayer today. Thank God for the specific things He's taught you. Confess where you fall short. Ask Him to continue to use this verse to make you more like Jesus!

_____

_____

_____

_____

_____

_____

_____

_____

_____

_____

_____

_____

_____

_____

_____

_____

_____

_____

_____

_____

_____

Viewer Guide

Watch the Session Three video. Use this page to take notes, capture quotes, or doodle some thoughts from the video teaching session.

Discussion Questions

Discuss the following questions with your Bible study group. A more extensive leader guide is available for free download at **LIFEWAY.COM/DWELL**.

1. What's one thing that stood out to you in this video teaching? Why?

2. At what point in time have you found it most difficult to rejoice? Difficult times? The mundane?

3. Who is the most joyful person you know? Why did you choose that person?

4. Why is joy essential to the Christian life?

5. How would you explain what it means to rejoice in the Lord?

6. How are you challenged by what you've heard in this video teaching?

7. Why is it so important for you to memorize this verse?

TO ACCESS THE VIDEO TEACHING SESSIONS, USE THE

INSTRUCTIONS IN THE BACK OF YOUR BIBLE STUDY BOOK.

Gentle and Near

session four

Quick Wins!

- Download the Scripture art to your phone, watch, or computer

- Watch the short memory verse video

- Apply the temporary verse tattoo found at the back of your Bible study book

SCRIPTURE ART DOWNLOAD

MEMORY VERSE: PHILIPPIANS 4:5

Or visit **LIFEWAY.COM/DWELL** for all memory verse videos and Scripture art downloads.

Set Up for Success

Let your gentleness be evident to all. The Lord is near. — Philippians 4:5

YOUR FIRST THOUGHTS

Before we start studying Philippians 4:5, let's take a first glance and see what we see.

What does this verse instruct us to do?

What does this verse tell us about the Lord?

What's your initial response to this verse? What does it make you think about? What emotions do you experience when you read the verse and why?

Instead of the word *gentleness*, the CSB translates it as *graciousness* and the ESV as *reasonableness*. How do all three translations help you understand what Paul meant for the Philippians to do?

How might our gentleness be related to Jesus's nearness?

How do you see this verse relating to the verses directly before and after it?

MY THOUGHTS

Gentleness. Sheesh.

Lately, I have not been gentle with my people. Rather, I've been short—short-fused, short in my responses, short in patience. And I know it. I see it. It's not that I don't want to be gentle. I do. I'm just not there right now.

So again, while this study is for you, it's also for me. I'm walking with you through this reality. I feel sure there have been times this week when you've been less than gentle in a conversation or an interaction with someone (even if only in your thoughts). Let's spend time in this verse and let it change us. Not just so we gain a gentle outer facade, but true gentleness in our hearts, thoughts, and actions toward others. Let's pursue an honest gentleness that comes from Jesus and pleases Him.

One other thing.

I want to figure out why Paul included that little statement "the Lord is near" To put a fire under us? Is it negative motivation for our gentleness—like Jesus is close by watching with a "tsk, tsk, tsk" whenever I'm not gentle? Or is the nearness of Jesus meant to be a positive motivation for our gentleness? Maybe it's just random—like a statement in an unrelated list? Whatever it is, I want to get to the bottom of it.

So, here's where we're headed this week.

Today, we're going to start work on the memorization part. (Be sure to put on your temporary tattoo!) In the next few days we'll start digging into the context and meaning behind those words we're learning. If we truly want to apply this verse to our lives, we've got to build our application on right understanding. That's what we want: right understanding, right application, and real heart change.

Daily Prayer

O God,

Thank You for Your Word. Thank You that You have goodness here for me in this verse. Open my heart and mind as I learn this verse and discover what it means.

Lord, I confess that I am not always gentle. Please forgive me for how I have not been gentle in these specific instances:

Lord, I also want to understand and long for Your nearness. I confess that my actions reveal I don't always want to be near You and spend time with You. Please forgive me for keeping You at arm's length in these specific moments:

Thank You, Lord, that You are a God who forgives all my sins and wanderings. Help me this week to learn about and long for Your gentleness. Thank You that You are near and always hear my prayers.

Amen

Evident Gentleness

Let your gentleness be evident to all. The Lord is near. — Philippians 4:5

GENTLENESS: THE NEW "CRUSHING IT"?

We stated earlier in the study that this Philippian passage is filled with commands. This verse is one of them.

I know that may seem obvious, but it's important to note because that means gentleness is not an option. It's mandatory—a rule for Christ followers on par with honoring our parents, loving our neighbors, and seeking justice for the oppressed. There's no room for excuses like "I'm sorry, that's just not my personality. I can't be gentle." Yet, I wonder if you look at gentleness the way I often do—a good quality, but optional (or at least not that important).

Why do you think we're so quick to devalue this command?

I think one reason, at least in part, is because gentleness is not seen as a virtue in our culture. Assertiveness is. Looking out for number one is. Crushing it like a boss lady is. But being gentle? That's for grandmas and doormats. We don't want anybody walking over us. Gentleness is for pushovers. How are we ever going to get ahead if we're gentle? Let's be real here.

But what if our culture is wrong about gentleness?

What if there's more to gentleness than meets the eye? What if there's a way to be strong and gentle at the same time? What if the inherent generosity and grace of gentleness is subversively winsome? What if being gentle is actually the best way to live? What if being gentle is crushing it? Since this is a command in Scripture, instituted for our thriving by the God who designed us, I have to believe that treating others with gentleness is all those things and more. Let's take a look.

WHAT'S THE POINT?

Let your gentleness be evident to all. The Lord is near.

PHILIPPIANS 4:5

Just like last week, we need to identify the focus points in our verse.

What focus points jump out at you?

Here are three I'd like us to explore:

- Letting our gentleness be known

- The nearness of the Lord

- How gentleness and nearness relate to each other and together fit into the passage

Here's a list of questions based on the focus points to guide us in our search for what this verse means:

- What is biblical gentleness, and what does it look like to let it be known to all?

- What's the meaning and significance of the nearness of the Lord?

- What do gentleness and the nearness of the Lord have to do with one another and how do they fit in the broader passage?

Let's look at the first question today.

LOOK IN THE BOOK

The Focus: Letting our gentleness be known

The Question: What is biblical gentleness, and what does it look like to let it be known to all?

Let's start by defining biblical gentleness. Here are two quick ways to do so:

1. **Read the verse in other Bible translations.**

2. **Look up *gentleness* in a Bible concordance. If you don't have a stack of Bibles in various translations or a Bible concordance, no worries! There are several free, easy-to-use resources online, such as biblegateway.com, blueletterbible.com, and biblehub.com.**

What different words are used for gentleness in other translations? (I gave you a couple yesterday. See page 62.)

What's the definition for gentleness from the online concordances?

From these sources, write your own definition of gentleness below.

Gentleness is the given word used in the NIV translation. But other translations use words like *graciousness*, *humility*, *reasonableness*, or *forbearance*. However you slice it, the idea is the same. Gentleness is considering others more highly than ourselves, not demanding our own rights but putting up with affronts, bearing patiently with the shortcomings of others, and treating others with grace. Whew! We're not just talking about your grandma's gentle hug here. We are talking about truly radical care for others.

You'll notice I didn't have you read other verses in this letter where Paul uses the word *gentle*. That's because he doesn't. So, is this a new command at the end of his letter? No. Just because the specific word *gentle* only occurs in 4:5, doesn't mean the theme of treating others with gentleness or graciousness isn't present elsewhere. As we consider the full definition of gentleness, this theme is evident throughout the letter.

Read Philippians 2:3-4 and Philippians 2:14-16. In the chart below, list ways we are and are not supposed to treat others.

TREAT OTHERS THIS WAY	DON'T TREAT OTHERS THIS WAY

How do these commands reflect the biblical definition of gentleness?

What do you think Paul meant by saying "you will shine among them like stars in the sky" (2:15)? How does this result of gentle behavior connect with our verse (4:5)?

Why is it important for us to let our gentleness be evident to all?

Who are some of the "all" you struggle to be gentle with?

Who is one person you need to show gentleness to today? In what specific ways will you display that gentleness?

When we look to the interests of others above our own, when we aren't seeking our own way or ambitions but those of others, it's so very winsome. Why? Because deep down, we all want to be treated like this. When someone gives up their prerogative or rights in order to serve us, it's shocking and attractive. Who is the best example of this quality? Jesus. It's how He's treated us. It's how we are to treat others. When we are gentle, we reflect Jesus. We're like lights in our dark world, pointing people to Him.

Daily Prayer

Dear Jesus,

Thank You for always being gentle with me. And You call me to be like You—gentle with others. It's one way I shine Your light in this dark world. Yet, so often I am not gentle. I think of myself first. I assert my rights. I don't consider others as I should. Forgive me for not being gentle in these specific situations:

Lord, thank You for always forgiving my failings and helping me live by the power of Your Spirit. Please help me show gentleness in these specific ways and with these specific people:

Jesus, thank You for letting me join in Your salvation work! Help me continue to see how my gentleness toward others is part of that work.

Amen

Understanding Nearness

Fill in the blanks:

Let_____ _____ be _____ to all.
The Lord _____ _____.

Philippians 4:5

NEAR AND DEAR?

I'll never forget what God taught me about how I read the Bible through this verse.

Several years ago, I was leading a Bible study at my church on this same passage in Philippians. When we got to this verse, one of the young moms shared something I didn't expect. She said the Lord's nearness had always sent a chill down her spine. She explained that she'd been raised to believe God was a strict judge—always watching and waiting for her to mess up, ready to punish her for her mistakes. The Lord's nearness was a source of fear and worry for her. I wanted to hug her and assure her, "No. The Lord isn't like that at all."

But then I wondered, "Could she be right?"

Although I didn't think so, perhaps *I* was the one reading it wrong. I wanted more than anything to tell her that she'd been misled, that the Lord is just and all-seeing, but He is also a God of mercy, kindness, and forgiveness. But here was the rub: at that point, it was my word against the teachers from her past. Why was my word any better than the teaching she'd received? How could we both know the right understanding of the Lord's nearness? The Scripture. We went to the Bible to figure out the true meaning of the Lord's nearness.

That's what we're going to do today.

Maybe you're like my friend, and you get a chill down your spine when you read about the nearness of the Lord. Or maybe that phrase brings you great comfort. We all have lenses we read the Bible through—experiences, culture, biases, upbringing, and teaching we've received (good or bad). Today, as much as we can, we're going to take off those lenses and read this verse in the context of this letter to discover what Paul meant by "The Lord is near."

LOOK IN THE BOOK

The Focus: The nearness of the Lord

The Question: What's the meaning and significance of the nearness of the Lord?

Throughout the story of Scripture, we see the Lord's heart to be near His people. In the beginning, God was near His children in unbroken fellowship in the garden of Eden. Even after their rebellion, He still longed to be near them. And the rest of the story of Scripture tells of God's ceaseless pursuit to be near His children—dwelling in the tabernacle and the temple, setting up the sacrificial system to provide a way for sinful people to come near Him, sending leaders to guide them in His ways and prophets to call them out of sin. God's desire to be near His children culminated in Christ—who became one of us, lived a holy life, and paid the price for our sins with His blood. This is the radical, wonderous nearness of our Lord. Let's read from another section of Paul's letter to discover more.

Read Philippians 2:5-11.

> What did Paul say about Jesus's status in verse 6? How did Jesus view His status?

> What did Jesus do to be near us and what was the cost?

> What did the obedience of Jesus in coming near achieve for us?

> When we think about Paul's command to be gentle, how do Jesus's actions described in this passage perfectly illustrate gentleness?

> Take a minute and reflect on what the gentle nearness of Jesus has meant to you. Journal some thoughts below.

Jesus came near us in gentleness, considering our needs above His own, not demanding His own rights, but treating us with undeserved mercy, not just overlooking our faults but paying the price for them. He came near for our good, for our salvation. He made a way for us to be reconciled to God.

His nearness is the very thing our hearts desire, the very thing our sin-soaked souls need. And now, He is near us for good, forever. He lives in us through the presence of the Holy Spirit, guiding us, comforting us, correcting us, and growing us in godliness.

Because of what Christ has done, God exalted Him and gave Him a name above every name. One day all knees will bow to Him and every tongue confess that Jesus Christ is Lord to the glory of God the Father. And we can confess this truth now. Jesus is Lord. And the Lord is near!

NEAR AND DEAR

By Natalie Abbott

Jesus—eternal, infinite, near—
Dwelt with us, one of us, became dear.
Gave up heaven to give all things.
Unmade Maker, made nothing,
Drank in-full the wrath-filled cup,
Willingly taking off and taking up:
Power for fragility,
Honor for humility,
Worship for a servant's towel,
Praise songs for our mocking scowl.
Humbled to the point of death.
Jesus gave His final breath.

Now He rules above all names,
And calls us to His great exchange:
He took off glory to take our sins,
Would we give our sins to Him?
Would our knees and tongues confess:
This Jesus is our righteousness?
If we do, we are His stars
Shining light into the dark.
And His mind become our own,
Loving others as He's shown.
To the far off, we come near.
So they too might become dear.

Daily Prayer

Dear Jesus,

You came near. Though You deserve only worship and praise and glory, You gave up all of these rights to put on flesh and take on my sin. I praise You and thank You for Your salvation, specifically in these ways:

Jesus, You came near, not in judgment, but in perfect gentleness. Lord, when I realize areas of sin in my life, please help me remember Your gentleness toward me. Please forgive my sin and help me know I don't have to hide or be afraid, but can come to You in repentance. Here are sins I need to confess today:

Lord, thank you for Your forgiveness. Help me apply this verse to my life, knowing You are near me all the time. Thank You for Your nearness in these circumstances especially:

Jesus, thank You that You are near even now.

Amen

How Does It All Relate?

Write out Philippians 4:5.

A RUDE INTRUDER OR THE GLUE?

Ok. Finally, we get to talk about what's been bothering me.

What does our gentleness have to do with Jesus being near? They seem unrelated to each other, right? And not only do these two concepts feel like an odd couple, if you read them in context, they don't feel cohesive with the flow of the passage. Let me elaborate.

First, write our verse from the last session, Philippians 4:4.

I hope these words are on the tip of your tongue. I hope this verse has anchored your soul to the joy of your salvation in Jesus. But what does rejoicing have to do with our displaying gentleness and Jesus's nearness? Moreover, if you read ahead to verse 6, Paul went straight into encouraging us to pray when we're anxious. Again, where's the tie in? What does gentleness and nearness have to do with anxiety?

Does the verse seem abrupt to you?

Here's something to keep in mind. When Paul wrote what we read as Philippians, he didn't sit down to write a book of the Bible, rather he was writing a letter to dear friends. Plus, the chapters and verse numbers in the letter were added centuries later. These reasons alone show the importance of reading this verse (and all of the Bible) in context.

So, while verse 5 might feel like that unknown guy who pushes into your group on a not-so-crowded train and makes everyone feel awkward, it's not out of place. As I dug in and really studied it, I started to see that this verse isn't a rude intruder but the glue that holds these ideas together. Paul knew exactly what he was doing when he wrote those two punchy little phrases, "Let your gentleness be evident to all. The Lord is near." Moreover, I wonder if his choppy phrasing (lacking linking words) was intentional. Maybe he wrote it that way so his original readers (and now us) would have to think about it, wrestle with it, and work hard to make the connections. Perhaps he meant for it to be relished and not rushed past. I personally think it's brilliant! Let's take a look.

LOOK IN THE BOOK

The Focus: How gentleness and nearness are related to each other and how they fit into the passage

The Question: What do gentleness and the nearness of the Lord have to do with one another and how do they fit in the broader passage?

Let's start off by examining the relationship of gentleness to Christ's nearness. To do so, look back at what we've studied the past two days from Philippians 2. First, we talked about our call to be gentle from Philippians 2:3-4 and 14-16. Then yesterday, we looked at Philippians 2:5-11 and noted how Jesus came near. Take a moment to review that passage.

What attitude characterizes the way in which Jesus came near?

How does this attitude correspond with the definition of gentleness we learned on Day Two?

How is our gentle treatment of others motivated by and linked to the nearness of Jesus?

Like we discussed on Day Three, we can be gentle with others because Jesus was gentle with us. He did not treat us as our sins deserved; He did not consider Himself, but us first. He humbly came near to bring us into relationship with the Father. And when we are gentle with others, we reflect the gentleness of Christ.

Who is someone you need to be more gentle with? How will you do so?

Now let's see how our verse fits in with the wider passage. I've formatted verses 4-7 below to see each separate thought and better understand how they relate.

> *4 Rejoice in the Lord always. I will say it again: Rejoice!*

> *5 Let your gentleness be evident to all. The Lord is near.*

> *6 Do not be anxious about anything, but in every situation, by prayer and petition, with thanksgiving, present your requests to God.*

> *7 And the peace of God, which transcends all understanding, will guard your hearts and your minds in Christ Jesus.*

How might the gentle nearness of Jesus impact our rejoicing in the Lord?

How might the Lord's nearness affect our ability to not be anxious about anything and our desire to bring everything to God in prayer?

What will be the result of giving our difficulties to the God who is near?

How do you think your life would be different in the coming week if you were constantly aware of the nearness of Christ?

The nearness of Christ is cause for rejoicing and urges us to call upon Him in our anxiousness. He is here for us. Close. Always.

Daily Prayer

Jesus,

I'm so grateful You are near. You are my reason for rejoicing! You are my motivation and the perfect example of gentleness. Thank You for how you have been gentle with me in this way:

Yet, Lord, I confess I sometimes push You away. I don't always rejoice in Your nearness or act gently toward all people. Forgive me, Jesus, for not allowing Your nearness to motivate me in these ways:

Jesus, as I become more aware of Your gentle nearness, help me to be more gentle and more present with others. Specifically, I want to be gentle and present in this circumstance with this person:

I praise You, Jesus. You are near. Please press that truth into my heart day by day as I recite this verse to myself and share it with others.

Amen

Gentle Nearness Applied

Write Philippians 4:4-5.

Ok friend, it's time to reflect on and respond to what you've learned this week. Use the following questions list to prompt your reflection.

- What are the most significant things you learned? What were your "aha moments," if any?

- Where did the Holy Spirit convict you while studying this verse?

- What changes do you need to make in your thoughts, attitudes, actions?

- How did your perspective of this verse change through the week as you studied it and meditated on it?

- In what situations and with what people do you need to be more gentle? Do you need to confess your harshness toward someone and ask for forgiveness? Explain.

- Write a letter to Jesus, thanking Him for the ways He has been close to you through a particular situation, past or present.

Reflections

Verses

FBAS

WIT
WIN
WIR

WIP
WIL
WIA

IAIEOPTAST
P4.8

WYHLOR
OHFM
SIM
PIIPAT
GOPW
BWY P4.9

lg
vg
bet
at
L
in p4.5

R
I
T
L
A
I
W
S
I
A
R
P
4
.
4

DNBAAAABIES
BPAPWT
PYRTG
P4.6

ATPOG WTAU WGYH AYM ICJ P4.7

Daily Prayer

Write your own prayer today. Thank God for the specific things He's taught you. Confess where you fall short. Ask Him to continue to use this verse to make you more like Jesus!

Viewer Guide

Watch the Session Four video. Use this page to take notes, capture quotes, or doodle some thoughts from the video teaching session.

Discussion Questions

Discuss the following questions with your Bible study group. A more extensive leader guide is available for free download at **LIFEWAY.COM/DWELL**.

1. What is one thing in the video teaching that stood out to you? Why?

2. How would you describe or define gentleness?

3. What keeps you from letting your gentleness be known to all?

4. How do you feel about the Lord's nearness? Is it comforting to you? Disconcerting? Explain.

5. How would you live differently if you were constantly aware that the Lord is near?

6. How are you challenged by what you've heard in this video teaching?

7. Why is it so important for you to memorize this verse?

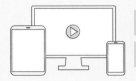

TO ACCESS THE VIDEO TEACHING SESSIONS, USE THE

INSTRUCTIONS IN THE BACK OF YOUR BIBLE STUDY BOOK.

Don't Be Anxious

Quick Wins!

Download the Scripture art to your phone, watch, or computer

Watch the short memory verse video

Apply the temporary verse tattoo found at the back of your Bible study book

SCRIPTURE ART DOWNLOAD

MEMORY VERSE: PHILIPPIANS 4:6

Or visit **LIFEWAY.COM/DWELL** for all memory verse videos and Scripture art downloads.

Set Up for Success

Do not be anxious about anything, but in every situation, by prayer and petition, with thanksgiving, present your requests to God. — Philippians 4:6

YOUR FIRST THOUGHTS

Before we start studying Philippians 4:6, let's consider our first impressions of the verse.

> What does this verse tell us about God?

> What does this verse tell us not to do? What does it tell us we should do?

> What's your initial response to this verse? What does it make you think about?

> Does it bother you that Paul is telling his friends (and consequently all believers) to not be anxious? Why or why not? Do you think that's even possible? Explain.

Have you ever given your anxiety to God as this verse instructs us to do? If so, describe your experience. If not, what kept you from doing so?

Are you anxious or worried about something right now? How are you handling the situation?

MY THOUGHTS

Talking about anxiety gives me anxiety.

Seriously. I suppose it's because anxiety is an old enemy I've battled for decades. It's all too real to me. It still takes me by surprise at inopportune moments, pursuing me, chasing me down, making my heart race and my breathing shallow. It turns my muscles to Jello®, ties my stomach in knots, and sits on my chest whispering worries and worst-case scenarios. Anxiety keeps me from rest and peace and joy. It lives in a box in my mind like a monster under my bed. I don't want to open that box and talk about it. Ever. I want to keep it contained. But, it never stays that way. It always finds a way to escape and attack again.

So, here we are.

I'm guessing you're familiar with what I'm talking about. Maybe reading my description of what anxiety feels like makes you feel a little anxious, even now. Maybe you don't like it either. Whether your anxiety is currently out of the box or sealed up tight, we need to talk about it, because God is talking to us about it in His Word.

If we are going to defeat this enemy, we need to open the box and go on the offensive.

I confess, I've only ever defended myself from anxiety when it's hitting me square in the face. I look up those "anxiety verses." I pray, and I ask for help, but only as a last resort. You may be thinking, "That sounds like a good plan of defense!" And sure, my reaction is helpful in the moment. But how much damage has been done to my emotions, my health, my relationships, my witness before I get to that point? Here's the thing: I've never once attacked anxiety when it wasn't already actively at work against me. I've never gone on the offensive. But that's what we are going to do this week. We're going to take anxiety out of that box and expose it to the full light of God's Word. We are going to identify its weaknesses and the best weapons to fight it so that before our next dark night, we'll be equipped and ready for the attack.

Are you willing to open that box?

Let's go to Jesus—our joy and our salvation who is near even now—and look in His Word to see what He has to say about our anxieties. I pray we will be emboldened in our hearts to give all our anxieties to Him.

ANXIETY IS . . .

By Natalie Abbott

A too-full chest, one breath from popping,
Yet through a straw, panting, sucking.
Heart is pounding, now I'm finding,
This pavement treadmill is revolving,
My feet are anchors barely moving,
Straining, striving for nowhere, nothing.
A spectacle for the growing mass—
Pointing, gaping, they soundlessly laugh.
Buildings cut off, threaten, bend.
I search upward for a super Man,
To bound the buildings and to bind,
This heavy heart I drag behind.
Will you lift me? Set me free?
Exchange peace for my anxiety?

Daily Prayer

O Jesus,

You are near. And You say I can give my worries to You. You have proven Yourself to me and given me so many reasons to trust You. Thank You for these specific reasons:

Lord, I have legitimate concerns, situations that are difficult, and problems that weigh me down and make my heart pound. Yet, I want to give my anxieties to You. Here's my list of what I'm anxious about:

Jesus, please help my anxious heart find its rest in You. Truly, You are my joy and my salvation. And You are near, hearing my prayers even now. Guide me as I learn from Your Word this week. Help me be honest about my worries and help me find ways to trust You with them. I know You are trustworthy; help me live that truth!

Amen

Honest Anxiety

Do not be anxious about anything, but in every situation, by prayer and petition, with thanksgiving, present your requests to God. — Philippians 4:6

ANXIETY: WHAT'S OK AND WHAT'S NOT OK

We all get anxious sometimes.

Times get hard. Something goes sideways. We receive bad news. We have an unexpected shortfall. Whatever the scenario, we're taken aback, uncertain, caught off guard. Our hearts quicken and our minds race as anxiety wells up in our bodies and our thoughts. Sometimes, if the situation gets better, the anxiety subsides, and we are right as rain. But what happens when the hard thing stays hard, the sideways situation doesn't get righted, the bad news gets worse, and the shortfall isn't met? Our anxiety stays too. Sometimes it sticks around long enough to become our new normal. For some of us, we develop a pattern of anxiety. It comes on even when there isn't any actual difficulty, just the possibility of it. Our minds race and our hearts beat like the perceived problem is an actual one. Whether our problem is authentic or perceived, whether it's constant or inconsistent, the anxiety is real.

I feel sure that's one of the reasons this verse is in the Bible.

Paul's friends had real anxiety, and he wanted to help them fight it. But they aren't the lone case of anxious people in the Bible, and this isn't the only verse on how to deal with it. Throughout Scripture we see God's children struggle again and again with honest worry. And in response, sometimes they sinned and sought godless solutions. Other times, they laid out their cares before God, the One who alone can save. (We see this most explicitly in the Psalms.) So, be encouraged! If the biblical saints struggled with anxiety, then it's fair to assume we're no different.

There's help for our anxiety!*

*NOTE: *While we're going to talk about a foundational way God helps us become free from our anxious thoughts and emotions, this study is by no means an exhaustive source on understanding anxiety or how to deal with it. Anxiety can range from situational worry to clinical anxiety. Regardless of the level of our anxiety, we're not meant to deal with it alone.*

We should seek God first, but also lean on our Christian community for help. We need friends to walk with us, pastors and elders to guide us and pray for us, and Christian counselors to expertly advise us when we need extra help. Don't hesitate to reach out.

While anxiety is part of the human experience in a fallen world, it's also awful. Am I right? Anxiety happens to all of us, but we don't want to stay anxious all the time. And in our worry, we don't want to wander from God. Instead, we want to cling to Him, the One who alone can free us from our anxiety. Paul's words can help us get that win.

Let's take a closer look at our verse and find the focus points we want to dig into and the questions we want to answer.

WHAT'S THE POINT?

> *Do not be anxious about anything, but in every situation, by prayer and petition, with thanksgiving, present your requests to God.*

> **PHILIPPIANS 4:6**

What focus points do you see in this verse?

Here are three for us to explore:

- We're not to be anxious about anything.

- The solution for anxiety: prayer.

- The right place for our anxiety: God.

These three ideas prompt three questions to guide our study of this verse:

- Is it possible to be concerned but not be anxious?

- How do we give everything to God in prayer?

- Why is coming to God with our worries the best thing we can do?

Let's get started with the first question.

LOOK IN THE BOOK

The Focus: We're not to be anxious about anything.

The Question: Is it possible to be concerned but not be anxious?

Let's examine a specific section of this letter that shows multiple people who are anxious or concerned.

> **Read Philippians 2:19-28.** List what each person was concerned about and make a note if their anxiety was real or perceived.

TIMOTHY	
EPAPHRODITUS	
PAUL	
THE PHILIPPIANS	

Let's take a closer look at what's said about Timothy. **Read verses 19-21 again.**

> *I hope in the Lord Jesus to send Timothy to you soon, that I also may be cheered when I receive news about you. I have no one else like him, who will show genuine concern for your welfare. For everyone looks out for their own interests, not those of Jesus Christ.*

In verse 20, the Greek word translated *genuine concern, merimnao,* **is the same word translated** *anxious* **in our memory verse (4:6).[1] What did Paul say about Timothy's concern? Is it good or bad?**

There are other instances in the New Testament where *merimnao* can have either a positive (1 Cor. 12:25) or a negative connotation (Luke 10:41). For an English comparison, think of how the word *fine* is used. A restaurant described as "fine dining" is where you expect to receive the choicest food and most excellent service. But if someone asked you about your experience at that restaurant and you described it as "fine," you would mean it was just ok or barely met the standard. In Philippians 2:20, it's clear Paul was speaking positively about Timothy's concern. But in our memory verse, Paul used the word in a negative light, telling the Philippians not to be anxious about anything. How can this be? What made Timothy's deep feelings different? Perhaps the answer was in Timothy's focus.

What was Timothy's primary focus (vv. 20-22)? How might this primary focus have kept his "genuine concern" from becoming the kind of anxiousness we should eliminate?

Evidently, Timothy's main interest was in Christ and advancing His kingdom. Timothy saw everything through that lens. This perspective would have allowed him to keep the right view of what was happening in the Philippian church. He entrusted them to the Lord and served them out of concern but not worry.

At what point do you think genuine concern becomes anxiety? How does that switch happen for you?

Do you currently have genuine concerns that tend to or have potential to become anxiety in you? Explain.

How might shifting your focus to Jesus alter how you see those specific concerns?

Let me remind you of something we alluded to earlier. As believers we're connected to a Christian community designed to help carry us through our difficult times. Paul didn't specifically mention that fact in this passage, but the spirit of it is found elsewhere in this letter (2:1-4) and his other letters (1 Cor. 12–13; Gal. 6:1-2).

How has your Christian community helped you through anxious times?

If you're not currently connected to such a community, what steps can you take to make that happen?

Just like Paul and his friends, we all have genuine concerns—situations that have the potential to make us anxious. But keeping our primary focus on the Lord and seeing things through that lens keeps genuine concern from escalating.

Daily Prayer

Dear Lord Jesus,

You are near, You hear me, and You care for me. I want to give You all my cares. Here are some of the things that I'm either worried about or tend to worry about:

Thank You, Jesus, for the Christian community that can help me through anxious times. Help me to either find or foster a community where we can share our honest burdens without shame or fear. Help me follow through with pursuing community in this way:

Thank You that You don't intend for me to walk through life or worry alone. You are good and Your intentions for me are good.

Amen

Practical Prayer

Fill in the blanks:

*Do not be _____ _____ _____, but in every
_____, by _____ _____ _____, with
_____, present your _____ _____ _____.*

Philippians 4:6

GIVING GOD ALL OF OUR EVERYTHING

In every situation, pray.

I don't know about you, but I have a lot of everything.

- People I love
- People I struggle with
- Difficult situations
- Easy situations
- Unknown situations
- All the things I'm responsible for
- Infinitely more things out of my control
- The future
- The past
- My dreams
- My nightmares
- My purpose
- All the possible and realized problems in the world
- All the possible and realized problems in my life

That's a lot of everything.

What about you? What's your everything? Does your list feel like a towering pile ready to topple over and crush you? Mine does sometimes. When we try to consider all of it at once, it's overwhelming and more than we can handle. It's no wonder our hearts race and our minds reel. We simply cannot deal with all of our everything. An honest assessment should lead any logical person to this realization: we are not wise enough, powerful enough, or good enough to take care of everything on our own. That's why Paul says to give it to God.

Give Him every single bit of it.

That massive, soul-crushing pile. Give it to God. He is wise enough. He is powerful enough. He is good enough. He can take care of your everything. He is the only right and safe place for all of it. Give it to Him.

But how?

Practically speaking, how do we give over our everything to God in prayer? Paul told us and showed us how. He shared some of his own anxieties in this letter and taught us by example how to give them to God. Let's take a look.

LOOK IN THE BOOK

The Focus: The solution for anxiety: prayer

The Question: How do we give everything to God in prayer?

> First, notice Paul's emphatic use of the most inclusive, absolute words to communicate what he meant. What aren't we supposed to be anxious about? What are we supposed to give to God in prayer? What are all the ways we should pray?

Paul used absolutes and repetition to emphasize his point. He said don't be anxious about *anything* and pray about *everything*. He mentioned four words to communicate how we are to come to God: prayer, petition, request, and thanksgiving. But this wasn't the only time he used absolutes and repetitive language to emphasize the importance of prayer.

Read Philippians 1:3-6 below.

> *I thank my God every time I remember you. In all my prayers for all of you, I always pray with joy because of your partnership in the gospel from the first day until now, being confident of this, that he who began a good work in you will carry it on to completion until the day of Christ Jesus.*

> Underline Paul's absolute statements. Circle where he used repetition. How do these literary devices emphasize the importance of prayer?

Although Paul emphasized how important prayer was, who did he say was in control of the outcome? What would the outcome be?

Paul wanted his readers to understand the full power of God over all things, and that God Himself would bring His good work to final, perfect, and absolute completion on the day Christ returns.

How does your concept of the power and significance of prayer align with Paul's?

Do you believe God has started a good work in you? How do you see Him at work in your life to complete that work?

Let's get back to the ways Paul told us to pray in our memory verse. The words *praying, petitioning,* and *presenting your requests* are similar in meaning. They all refer to coming to God and asking Him to help. We are to take our anxieties (and everything else) to God and ask Him to take care of them. Our prayers don't have to be fancy or prescribed; we just present Him with what's heaviest upon our hearts, believing that He is going to bring good out of our situations. We believe He will complete His good work in us despite the difficulties we face.

Are you able to pray this way when you're anxious? If so, how? If not, why not?

When you think about it, praying with thanksgiving in anxious times seems oddly timed. When do we normally thank God in prayer?

How is praying with expectant thanksgiving related to being confident that God will bring the good work He started to completion (like we saw in Phil. 1:4-6)?

How might you incorporate this kind of thankful praying into your life during anxious times?

Keep in mind we're not instructed to necessarily be thankful for the difficult circumstances we're in that bring us anxiety. Rather, we're to be thankful for the Lord's presence and peace. Thankful that He's got us and is for us and will carry us through whatever we're facing. And thankful that whatever the outcome, it will be for our good and His glory (Rom. 8:28).

Daily Prayer

Dear God,

Thank You for being wise, powerful, and good. You are in control of everything, including all of my everything. I praise You for all the ways I've seen You answer these specific prayers in my life:

In light of Your providence, You would think I would trust You all the time, but so often I do not. Forgive me for remaining crushed under the weight of these worries:

Lord, I confess these worries to You and thank You for your presence, Your forgiveness, and Your peace. I trust You to bring to completion the good work You have started in me.

Thank You that I don't have to be anxious about anything because You have everything under control and destined for a good end.

Amen

The Right Place for Anxiety

Write out Philippians 4:6.

AM I CONFIDENT IN GOD?

That's the question we're asking today.

All this information, everything we've learned so far—none of it matters if we don't live like it. There's no value in it if we still get up every morning and live like these truths aren't real, like Jesus doesn't care, that He isn't present, available, near, ready to listen to our every prayer about our everything.

We can know all the answers and still live like we don't.

So, I have to ask, are you truly putting your confidence in God—moment by moment, believing that He cares and He's listening? Do you trust Him with your anxieties? Are you confidently *praying* or do you just *know* that you should? Do you confess Jesus is near but live like He's far away or relegated to a church building, only available on Sundays?

Paul said not to do this.

Throughout his letter Paul was persistently confident that God would come through for him despite every possible source of anxiety. He modeled for us what he commanded us to do in our verse this week. He showed us how we can be confident in every request we make to God. Let's jump right in.

LOOK IN THE BOOK

The Focus: The right place for our anxiety: God

The Question: Why is bringing our worries to God the best thing we can do?

We already know that Paul had a lot to be anxious about. But what about his confidence? Was he confident God would come through for him?

I just read through Philippians with an eye on Paul's confidence in God. Wow. You've got to do this also! It's so evident that Paul had full trust in God. We're not going to read the whole letter today with that theme in mind. However, I've selected a few of the passages that make Paul's confidence amazingly clear!

How did Paul express his confidence in the Lord in the following passages in Philippians?

1:4-6	
1:12-14	
1:20-26	
2:24	
3:8-9	
3:20-21	
4:12-13	
4:19	

Ok. Let's do a recap of how Paul expressed his confidence in the Lord.

- Paul was confident God completes every good work He starts.

- Paul was confident God was working through his difficult circumstances.

- Paul was confident in God's purpose for him whether he lived or died.

- Paul was convinced he would live on to encourage his friends, so they could boast about what Christ had done.

- Paul was "confident in the Lord" about his travel plans.

- Paul placed his confidence not in the flesh but in the righteousness of Christ.

- Paul was sure of his security in Christ and in the promised reward that awaited him.

- Paul confidently awaited the return of Jesus and the transformation of his old body into a glorious new body through the power of Christ.

- Paul was confident he could do anything through Christ who strengthened him.

- Paul knew God would abundantly provide for every need of His people.

WHOA! This is extreme confidence! What can we learn from Paul? We can be confident not in our own performance or strength or ability, but in God's. We can be confident in our God—who delivers, who finishes every good work, who won't leave us ashamed, but who gives us courage and righteousness, who we will one day meet in glory and who meets our every need in the meantime. This is our God, and He alone is worthy of all our confidence. Surely, we can give Him all our everything in prayer.

Which of Paul's expressions of confidence in God did you most need to hear today and why?

How does the confidence Paul expressed give you confidence in God for a specific situation you're dealing with?

Let all these wonderful truths build your confidence in God. Doing so will allow you to bring to Him that massive pile of all your everything we talked about yesterday and trust Him with it. He is faithful. He is trustworthy. He will never fail you.

Daily Prayer

O God,

You are so, so good. Thank You for all the ways You are worthy of my confidence. Specifically, I'm so grateful that You are:

Despite all I know about You, too often, I don't live like I'm confident in Your purpose, power, or presence. Forgive me for my doubt and help me have confidence in You in this specific situation:

Lord, I believe in You and all the reasons I have to trust You. Please help me be more confident in my prayer life in this specific way:

Lord, my hope and confidence are in You.

Amen

Prayer Applied

Write all the verses you've learned so far. If you need more space, feel free to use the Reflections page!

Ok friend, it's your turn to reflect on and respond to what you've learned this week. Use the following questions as prompts.

- What are the most significant things you learned? What were your "aha moments," if any?

- Where did you feel convicted by this verse?

- What changes do you need to make in your thoughts, attitudes, actions?

- How did your perspective of this verse change through the week as you studied it and meditated on it?

- How can you foster Christian friendships like Paul had?

- Write out a list of "all of your everything." Then evaluate your list: Which items can you describe as "genuine concerns" and which of them are currently causing you anxiety? What is one truth about God that gives you confidence to entrust each of those worries to Him?

- Write out an expectantly thankful prayer.

- Look back at your "all of your everything" list. What is one item on the list you tend to always worry about? What can you practically do to create a pattern of giving that issue to God every time that worry surfaces?

Reflections

Verses

FBAS

WIT
WIN
WIR

WIP
WIL
WIA

IAIEOPTAST
P4.8

WYHLOR
OHFM
SIM
PIIPAT
GOPW
BWY P4.9

R
I
T
L
A
I
W
S
I
A
P4.4

I
vg
bet
at
L
in
p4.
5

DNBAAABIES
BPAPWT
PYRTG
P4.6

ATPOG WTAU WGYH AYM ICJ P4.7

Daily Prayer

Write your own prayer today. Thank God for the specific things He's taught you. Confess where you fall short. Ask Him to continue to use this verse to make you more like Jesus!

Viewer Guide

Watch the Session Five video. Use this page to take notes, capture quotes, or doodle some thoughts from the video teaching session.

Discussion Questions

Discuss the following questions with your Bible study group. A more extensive leader guide is available for free download at **LIFEWAY.COM/DWELL**.

1. What's one thing that stood out to you in this video teaching? Why?

2. Do you think it's possible to not be anxious about anything? Explain.

3. What's the difference in genuine concern and anxiousness?

4. In what area of life do you most often spiral down from concern to anxiousness? Explain.

5. How are you able to pray with thanksgiving in all the anxious things you're to give to God?

6. How are you challenged by what you've heard in this video teaching?

7. Why is it so important for you to memorize this verse?

TO ACCESS THE VIDEO TEACHING SESSIONS, USE THE

INSTRUCTIONS IN THE BACK OF YOUR BIBLE STUDY BOOK.

Safe Hearts and Minds

session six

Quick Wins!

- Download the Scripture art to your phone, watch, or computer

- Watch the short memory verse video

- Apply the temporary verse tattoo found at the back of your Bible study book

ATPOG WTAU WGYH AYM ICJ P4.7

SCRIPTURE ART DOWNLOAD

MEMORY VERSE: PHILIPPIANS 4:7

Or visit **LIFEWAY.COM/DWELL** for all memory verse videos and Scripture art downloads.

Set Up for Success

ATPOG WTAU WGYH AYM ICJ P4.7

And the peace of God, which transcends all understanding, will guard your hearts and your minds in Christ Jesus. — Philippians 4:7

YOUR FIRST THOUGHTS

Before we start studying Philippians 4:7, let's take a first glance.

What does this verse tell us about God?

What's your initial response to this verse? What does it make you think about?

What do you think it means that God's peace transcends understanding?

How would you describe a heart and mind guarded by peace?

What do you think it means to be "in Christ Jesus"? And why is that phrase so important to the promise in this passage?

MY THOUGHTS

God's peace.

Peace that transcends understanding.

Peace that guards my heart, my every feeling.

Peace that protects my mind, my every thought.

Peace that is found in Jesus Christ.

I want that kind of peace. I need that kind of peace.

How about you? Real peace. Peace that baffles and confounds logic. Peace to calm your fickle feelings and stay your spinning mind. Peace to free you from all your worries and anxieties. This is the peace that comes when we give our anxieties to God in prayer. It is a peace that makes no sense, a peace that can't be explained, a peace we have in Christ, and it is always available to us when we pray. This is the promise of our verse.

And it is so, so good.

I can attest to it. Last week, I needed this peace like nobody's business. I'll spare you the details, but my day-in and day-out experience was one of intermittent anxious thoughts and feelings. More than anything, I needed peace. I needed freedom from that old enemy, anxiety.

So, what did I do?

Some simple things—I read my Bible and journaled about my feelings. I asked a couple of close friends to pray for me and with me. And in those hectic moments when the anxious feelings and thoughts hit me throughout the day, I took a deep breath and recited the verses we've been memorizing (including this week's verse). Then I gave my anxiety over to God in prayer.

God met me in those moments.

He was near. He heard my prayers. He gave me peace. And He is meeting me still, even now. Whenever I feel that anxiety rising in my chest, I keep doing what I've been doing, reciting these verses and giving my burdens to my Father. I confess, my problems and anxieties didn't go away with a snap of my fingers. No, I haven't arrived at constant perfect peace, but I do experience it regularly, moment by moment. Such peace is a gift from God—a gift He wants to give you too.

Daily Prayer

Lord God,

Thank You for being near me and hearing me when I pray. Thank You for giving my heart and mind peace when I pray to You. Thank You for giving me peace in this specific situation:

Lord, I confess that I often fall short of living in the peace that You offer. I sometimes try to control my situation, find my own solutions, and not trust You with it. Please forgive me for not seeking Your peace through prayer in these specific times:

Help me apply this verse to my life this week.

Thank You for Your peace. I know I so desperately need it. Help me seek and find You and Your peace today.

Amen

The Peace of God

And the peace of God, which transcends all understanding, will guard your hearts and your minds in Christ Jesus. — Philippians 4:7

A PEACE LIKE THAT

When I think of peace, I think of my friend Anita.

I'll never forget a conversation I had with her about her heart condition, which was brought on by an illness when she was a missionary kid in Africa. The condition required surgery. As she shared, I realized the significance of the situation, the danger she faced, and the necessity for the procedure. But she talked about it like she was having a wart removed, like it was no big deal. But it was a big deal. I couldn't help but ask her how she could be so peaceful. She responded that God, who had always taken care of her in life, would take care of her even in her death. It was apparent she had the peace of God.

> **Do you know someone who displays this kind of peace? If so, who? How is God's peace apparent in that person's life?**

God's peace makes no earthly sense. It's a peace not dependent on circumstances. In fact, we can experience His peace despite real and rational reasons for anxiety. His peace goes above and beyond our solutions and control, our abilities and strategies, our striving and grasping. It exceeds our finite limits and transcends our possibilities.

In all our earthly troubles, we can experience peace from God. In fact, just before Jesus left this earth, He told His disciples,

> *Peace I leave with you; my peace I give you. I do not give to you as the world gives. Do not let your hearts be troubled and do not be afraid.*

> JOHN 14:27

This is not a worldly kind of peace and not just an absence of conflict or difficulty. It's a heavenly peace, one that unburdens and protects our troubled hearts and minds. This is the peace we're examining in our study today—the promised peace of God when we pray.

WHAT'S THE POINT?

And the peace of God, which transcends all understanding, will guard your hearts and your minds in Christ Jesus.

PHILIPPIANS 4:7

What are some focus points in this verse?

Here are two that stand out to me:

- The peace of God

- Safe hearts and minds

Let's look at two questions that relate to these focus points and a third question that relates to the greater passage.

- What is the peace of God?

- What does it mean to have safe hearts and minds?

- How does this verse tie in with all the other verses we've learned so far?

LOOK IN THE BOOK

The Focus: The peace of God

The Question: What is the peace of God?

This question spawns more questions in my mind: How do we get the peace of God? Who receives God's peace? What is God's peace like? Let's take a look at these questions.

1. **How do we get the peace of God?**

Review last week's verse and lesson to help answer this question. What are we exchanging for God's peace?

God Himself, who hears our prayers and cares about our anxiety, gives us peace when we come to Him in prayer.

In Philippians 4:7, how is God's peace described and what does this peace do for us?

2. Who receives God's peace?

Notice that little phrase "in Christ Jesus" at the end of Philippians 4:7. The protective peace of God is contingent on us being "in Christ Jesus." But what does that phrase mean? Let's find out!

Thankfully, Paul used that phrase liberally throughout his letters. Let's look at some examples in Philippians.

What do each of these verses tell us about what it means to be "in Christ"?

PHILIPPIANS 1:1	
PHILIPPIANS 3:8-9	
PHILIPPIANS 3:14	

We can have peace from our anxiety because we first have peace with God in Christ. Philippians 1:1 calls us "holy people [or saints] in Christ Jesus." That doesn't mean we're spiritually elite or our goodness stands above others. Our status is totally dependent on Christ and what He has done for us. We are "found in Him" because of His righteousness, which is granted to us through faith. So, we can have peace in the midst of our troubles, because we know "in Christ" we have everything we need. Our salvation is secure in Christ, and every good gift of God (including His peace) is also found in Him. Thus it's fitting for all believers to be referred to as being "in Christ Jesus" and for all our blessings also to be found "in him." Conversely, there is no good thing found outside of Him (Jas. 1:17). Therefore, as we learned in Session Three, we can and should "rejoice in the Lord always!"

How do these verses shed light on what we can know about the peace of God? If our peace is dependent on our salvation "in Christ Jesus," how can we know that peace is secure?

3. **What is God's peace like?**

Look up Philippians 4:7 in other translations.

What are different ways the phrase "transcends all understanding" is translated in other Bible versions?

Describe in your own words what it means that the peace of God transcends understanding.

God's peace surpasses or transcends or exceeds our ability to conceive it. His peace goes beyond what our limited minds can understand. Frankly, peace is never a logical human response to our anxiety-producing circumstances. To have peace in the face of anxiety is otherworldly and incomprehensible.

Left totally up to you, how would you handle something that makes you anxious? How does God's peace transcend or exceed what you can imagine or control?

In what anxious situation have you experienced the baffling peace of God?

What is one worrisome thing you repetitively deal with? Are you struggling to give it to God in prayer? If so, how are you trying to manage it or control it by your own understanding? What's keeping you from giving it to God instead?

Daily Prayer

Dear God,

Thank You for the peace You give me in Jesus through His saving work on my behalf! Thank You for the peace You provide me in these areas of my life:

Though I want to trust You for Your peace, I confess I often seek my own understanding instead of Your peace that transcends it. Please forgive me for following my own limited knowledge in these situations:

Please give me Your otherworldly peace in exchange for these things that make me anxious:

Thank You for providing a way for me to live in peace every day, in every situation.

Amen

Truly Safe

Fill in the blanks:

And the _____ _____ _____, which _____ _____
_____, will guard _____ _____ _____ _____
_____ in _____ _____.

Philippians 4:7

WHAT'S YOUR SECURITY BLANKET?

When I was a kid, I always made a running leap to get into bed.

Why? Leaping got me past the under-the-bed monster, of course. Maybe your experience was similar to mine. I tried my best to avoid the fearsome beast—the one with the long arms who was always waiting in that deep darkness, ready to grab my ankles and pull me down into the black. Once safely in bed, I would settle in under the covers as deep as I could, even covering my head (a habit I've never broken), in order to protect myself from that fearful enemy. In my childish understanding, those pulled-up blankets kept me safe. I laugh now as an adult, knowing both the threat and the solution were equally false.

But truth be told, things haven't changed much. I still have blankets I hide under.

What about you? What blankets are you hiding under?

Where are your go-to safe places? I'm not talking physically, but mentally and emotionally? Where do you go when your heart and mind are askew? I'm not asking where you should go. You probably know the "right" answer, the one you hopefully, eventually arrive at. I want the real answer, your actual response when things get tough. Do you avoid the problem—watching shows and scrolling your socials? Do you face situations head on—making plans, writing up lists, figuring out possible solutions? Do you spin your gears—going down internet rabbit holes, wondering if you'll ever get out?

Me? I'm the classic avoider. I will do *literally anything* other than "go there" and deal with my anxious thoughts and feelings. That's my real answer. But avoidance doesn't actually help. You probably feel the same about your honest answer. Deep down we know none of these self-reliant actions protect our hearts and minds. They're false security blankets, unable to help us when life feels scary.

But we know the right answer.

We've already discovered that when we choose not to wallow in our anxiousness but present our worries to God in prayer He gives us His peace. Today we're going to discover why going there is the safest place for our reeling minds and hurting hearts. But we don't want to just learn this truth, we want to lean into it and live it out. That way, the next time we find ourselves curled up under a security blanket, we can recognize our folly, and throw it off in exchange for the real safety of God's protective peace.

LOOK IN THE BOOK

The Focus: Guarded hearts and minds

The Question: What does it mean to have safe hearts and minds?

The word *guard* is a military term.[1] Paul also used this term in 2 Corinthians 11:32 to speak of the soldiers who were guarding Damascus in order to arrest him. Yet, Paul was talking about peace in verse 7. We already know this peace boggles the mind, but here Paul described a seeming paradox.

How do you think the peace of God is like a military force?

I love this picture of the peace of God being powerful and able to protect us! When we give our anxieties to the Lord, His peace surrounds our hearts and minds like a military force guarding a city to keep out the enemy. The peace of God keeps out those thoughts that cause us to worry and fret. He calms our hearts and minds and helps us think rightly about the anxious situations. How? It's unexplainable, according to the verse. Fortunately, we don't have to fully understand it to rest in it.

How does this explanation give you courage and hope?

Let's find out more about what the Scripture has to say about the two things under attack: our hearts and minds (our emotions and our thought lives).

Read Proverbs 4:23 below to see a biblical concept of the heart.

Above all else, guard your heart, for everything you do flows from it.

Rewrite this verse in your own words.

How does this verse show the importance of our hearts being guarded?

Read Romans 12:1-2 to see the importance of having a guarded mind.

What is a mind both transformed and renewed by God's Word able to do?

There are times in the Bible we see the heart (emotions) and mind (thoughts) paired together to indicate the whole person (Deut. 11:18). In fact, some scholars say that's what Paul was doing in Philippians 4:7.[2] What we think and how we feel certainly impact one another and are central to who we are as people. Let's look at what Paul has to say about the interrelational nature of our thoughts and feelings.

Read Philippians 1:9-11.

How did Paul speak of the relationship between emotions and thoughts (v. 9)?

What would be the result of emotions rooted in knowledge and insight (vv. 10-11)?

Read Philippians 2:1-2. How do these verses show emotions and thoughts intertwined? How is Christian unity dependent on both the thought life and the emotional life?

When our thoughts are renewed, our lives are transformed. When our emotions are rooted in knowledge and insight, we can discern and act on what's best, experience the fruit of righteousness, and bring glory to God!

How does this profound significance related to our hearts and minds raise the importance of Philippians 4:6-7? Why are these parts of our being worth guarding?

How does this understanding further motivate you to take your worries to God in prayer?

I'm glad we're no longer worried about the imaginary monsters under the bed. However, our world can still be a frightening place, filled with decisions, situations, and circumstances that chill our hearts and keep our minds fretting. Through prayer, let's continually reach for the security blanket of God's transcendent peace to cover and guard us.

Daily Prayer

O God,

Thank You for Your Word that reveals truth to me. Thank You for this specific truth I learned today about my heart and mind:

Lord, I confess that I often don't bring You my anxious thoughts and feelings in prayer. Forgive me for relying on these false security blankets instead of You:

Lord, thank You for guarding my heart and my mind with Your peace. When anxious thoughts or feelings crop up, please remind me by Your Spirit to give them to You.

Amen

Making the Connections

ATPOG WTAU WGYH AYM ICJ P4.7

Write out Philippians 4:7.

THERE'S ALWAYS MORE!

God's Book is different.

I read a lot. I love all the words. I love poetry and prose and fiction and nonfiction. I even love the smell of a book and the feel of one in my hand. I have reread books multiple times for the sheer love of them. But the Bible is different from any book I've ever read. I've read it, reread it, read books about it, studied it, memorized it, and yet I never tire of it. In fact, the more I learn of it, the more I love the Bible and am increasingly astounded at its beauty and complexity and cohesion and depth. If I spent a thousand years in Scripture, I would only want a thousand more. God's Book is like no other.

Why do I tell you all of that?

Because we're wrapping up our first section of verses and I'm overwhelmed with the brilliance of the whole paragraph. And just so you know, much of what we're going to look at today (and everything else we're learning in this study), was filtered through the scholarly lens of commentaries written about this passage.

Let's take a look.

LOOK IN THE BOOK

The Question: How does this verse tie in with all the other verses we've learned so far?

To see how all our verses relate to one another, we're going to examine two brilliant literary techniques Paul used that we touched on in Session Five, Day Three: absolutes and repetition. First we'll look at how he used the repetition of absolutes for emphasis, and then, second, we'll see how he used repeated words to highlight a contrast.

Repetition of Absolutes

Write out each of the following verses (from memory, if you can!). Then look for the absolutes (indicated by words like always, anything, all, and every). Note: in the original Greek language, the words translated *all*, *always*, and *every* have the same root word *pas*, making the repetition more evident to the original first century readers.[3]

> Write Philippians 4:4. What's the absolute statement?

> Write Philippians 4:5. Again, what's the absolute statement?

> Write Philippians 4:6. What are the two absolute statements?

> Write Philippians 4:7. What's the absolute statement?

To show you the force these words give to the meaning of this text, I've rewritten the verses without them. **Read the verses below** and see how differently they land.

> *Rejoice in the Lord. I will say it again: Rejoice! Let your gentleness be evident. The Lord is near. Do not be anxious, but in situations, by prayer and petition, with thanksgiving, present your requests to God. And the peace of God, which transcends understanding, will guard your hearts and your minds in Christ Jesus.*

How does the loss of the absolutes change the meaning of the verses? Does the message seem more or less impactful or important? Explain.

For me, these verses land flat without the absolutes. Though much of the meaning is retained, the urgency and emphasis are lost. The original language reads as if Paul was leaning across the table, almost too close, with hope-filled eyes and a choked up voice. He's desperate to communicate just how significant it is to live like this—to rejoice in the Lord always, to be gentle with all people and anxious about nothing, giving every situation to God in prayer and experiencing the peace that transcends all understanding. This was the way Paul deeply desired all God's people to live, including you and me.

Are you living this way? Is this your current experience? If so, describe some of the details. If not, why not? What needs to change for you to get there?

Repetition for Contrast

Paul wasn't concerned about the risk of repeating himself. In this short passage, he did so for contrast. Again, his repetition would've been more noticeable in the original Greek, but a bit harder to pick up in our English translations (including the NIV). It's a little more noticeable in the ESV.

Read verses 5 and 6 below and circle the repeated words.

> *Let your reasonableness be known to everyone. The Lord is at hand; do not be anxious about anything, but in everything by prayer and supplication with thanksgiving let your requests be made known to God.*

> PHILIPPIANS 4:5-6 (ESV)

The words translated *be known* and *be made known* are similar in the original Greek.[4]

What two things are we to make known and to whom?

Paul could've said, "Be gentle to all people" and "pray to God." But he didn't. Instead he used repetitive words to force a contrast between what we make known to others with what we make known to God.

Who gets our best behavior and who sees all our hard realities?

How might praying about our hard situations help us be gentle with all people, even the difficult people who might cause some of our anxiety?

How do you need to reorient the ways you're treating those around you? And how do you need to reorient what you're praying about and in what attitude?

Friend, I really hope these verses are settling into your heart. I hope today's deeper study of them has strengthened your understanding and reliance on them. Right now I feel like what I imagine Paul felt. I'm leaning in with tears and hope-filled eyes, begging you to make this beautiful way of living your own. You can do this! You can recite these verses—the very words of God—as you lay out your own anxious thoughts and feelings before Him. Let God show up for you in the middle of your mess and the middle of the night to reassure you that He is near, that He cares, and that He wants all of you—all your worries, rejoicing, prayers, and gratitude. He is the only good and safe place for your heart and mind.

Daily Prayer

O Jesus,

You are gentle and near, kind and caring, here and hearing. I love You so much. Help me love You more. Help these verses sink deep in my heart and mind. I want to especially thank You for this life-changing truth:

Lord, I confess I don't always apply what I'm learning. But I want to do so! I want to rejoice and be gentle and prayerful. I want to experience Your peace! Please forgive me for the following ways I have failed at this in the recent past:

Now Jesus, I pray, by the power of Your Spirit, that You would help me take the following steps to live out these truths:

Lord Jesus, I rejoice in You right now. Hear my prayer and give me Your peace.

Amen

Peace Applied

Write all the verses you've learned so far. If you need more space, feel free to use the Reflections page!

Ok friend, it's your turn to reflect on and respond to what you've learned this week. Use the following questions as prompts.

- What are the most significant things you learned? What were your "aha moments," if any?

- Where did you feel convicted by this verse?

- What changes do you need to make in your thoughts, attitudes, actions?

- How did your perspective of this verse change through the week as you studied it and meditated on it?

- Would you consider yourself a worrier? Explain.

- Is the peace of God guarding your heart and mind right now? If not, why not?

- How have you experienced the transcendent peace of God in the past?

- How has Philippians 4:4-7 impacted your view of prayer?

- What is one action step you want to take to incorporate what you learned this week?

Reflections

Verses

FBAS

WIT
WIN
WIR

WIP
WIL
WIA

IAIEOPTAST
P4.8

WYHLOR
OHFM
SIM
PIIPAT
GOPW
BWY P4.9

R
I
T
L
A
I
W
S
I
A

R

P4.4

I
yg
bet
aL
in
p4.
5

DNBAAABIES
BPAPWT
PYRTG

P4.6

ATPOG WTAU WGYH AYM ICJ P4.7

Daily Prayer

Write your own prayer today. Thank God for the specific things He's taught you. Confess where you fall short. Ask Him to continue to use this verse to make you more like Jesus!

Viewer Guide

Watch the Session Six video. Use this page to take notes, capture quotes, or doodle some thoughts from the video teaching session.

session six

Discussion Questions

Discuss the following questions with your Bible study group. A more extensive leader guide is available for free download at **LIFEWAY.COM/DWELL**.

1. What's one thing that stood out to you in this video teaching? Why?

2. Do you think living in this peace of God is a reality or is it an unattainable hope? Explain.

3. How does our desire to control things counteract the instructions and promise of this verse and the previous verse?

4. Describe a time when you experienced the peace of God that transcends all understanding.

5. How does God's peace guard your heart and mind in Christ Jesus?

6. How are you challenged by what you've heard in this video teaching?

7. Why is it so important for you to memorize this verse?

TO ACCESS THE VIDEO TEACHING SESSIONS, USE THE

INSTRUCTIONS IN THE BACK OF YOUR BIBLE STUDY BOOK.

We're Never Not Thinking

session seven

Quick Wins!

- Download the Scripture art to your phone, watch, or computer

- Watch the short memory verse video

- Apply the temporary verse tattoo found at the back of your Bible study book

SCRIPTURE ART DOWNLOAD

MEMORY VERSE: PHILIPPIANS 4:8

Or visit **LIFEWAY.COM/DWELL** for all memory verse videos and Scripture art downloads.

Session Seven: We're Never Not Thinking   137

Set Up for Success

Finally, brothers and sisters, whatever is true, whatever is noble, whatever is right, whatever is pure, whatever is lovely, whatever is admirable—if anything is excellent or praiseworthy—think about such things. — Philippians 4:8

YOUR FIRST THOUGHTS

Let's take a first glance at this verse and see what we see.

What's your initial response to this verse?

What does this verse encourage you to do? What might be the result if you lived this out?

What questions do you have about this verse?

Would you say this list of virtues is what dominates your thought life? If not, why not? What does dominate your thoughts?

How might your life change if you did think on these things most of the time?

How does the word *finally* affect the way you read this verse?

MY THOUGHTS

I'm never not thinking.

And neither are you. Whether we realize it or not, our minds are constantly at work. Every minute of every hour of every day. In fact, we sometimes have trouble sleeping because we can't seem to shut down our minds as they wallow in worry or race down every possible path. Even while we're sleeping our minds rummage through the fodder of our days and fabricate strange stories that baffle us upon waking. We are a constantly thinking, thought-filled people.

And the thoughts we think really matter.

So, of course, God, through Paul, has something to say about this reality. Paul, who encouraged us to rejoice, admonished us to be gentle, reminded us of Christ's nearness, and commanded us to exchange our anxieties for peace, now tells us what to think about.

Are you at all surprised? I'm not.

Paul was just that guy. We can count on his teaching to tell us what's what. But, at this point, we also know his tender heart for God's people and his desire to see goodness multiplied in our lives. So, since Paul said, "think about such things," I want to think about them! Moreover, I want to know why I should think about these things. That desire means I'm ready to lean in and explore Paul's emphatic, exhaustive list of proper thoughts.

Here's the list: whatever is true, noble, right, pure, lovely, admirable, excellent, or praiseworthy. Whew! That's a lot. But isn't this list of virtues the very thing we want for our thought lives? Aren't we worn out from dwelling on all the negative things? Don't we want to have a mind filled with what is true and right and lovely? Yes and amen!

All the time.

Paul wasn't telling us to think on these things some of the time, but constantly. We discovered in Session Two, Day Three that the word *think* in the original Greek is in the present tense, which indicates ongoing action. Therefore, we're supposed to *continually* be thinking on these things! As we've said, our minds never take a break. Unfortunately, they tend to fixate on our anxieties. So, let's start giving our minds something better to dwell on—what's true and right and lovely and praiseworthy!

Daily Prayer

Dear God,

Thank You for my mind and for how it can learn and process information. Please, by Your Spirit, train my mind to think on the following godly things:

Lord, too often I don't dwell on what's good. Instead I'm prone to think on negative and even sinful things. Please forgive me for thinking on these wrong things:

Lord, thank You for Your forgiveness and please help my thoughts reflect these godly virtues. Here's one virtue from the list I want to specifically dwell on today and why:

More than anything, help me desire and work for the kind of thought life You've created me for and want me to have.

Amen

Thinking About Our Thoughts

Finally, brothers and sisters, whatever is true, whatever is noble, whatever is right, whatever is pure, whatever is lovely, whatever is admirable—if anything is excellent or praiseworthy—think about such things. — Philippians 4:8

DWELL ON THESE THINGS

I cried in the shower this morning.

I just let it all out to God—a long exhale of all the things weighing me down. I let go of everything out of my control, all of the ways I've failed and floundered, all of my long-term hard prayers. I sobbed before God and made my requests. After I finished, I felt His peace. I really did.

But then, I had a choice to make.

What was I going to fill my head and heart with going forward? Was I going to keep circling my thoughts on those hard things or refocus my thoughts to the good things of God? Was I going to dwell on what was false or what was true? On how things had gone wrong or how God could make it right? On what had been spoiled or trust God who makes all things pure? What lens was I going to choose to see the world through today? So, I recited Philippians 4:8. I asked God to help me focus on Him and His good things instead of giving into the temptation to jump back onto the anxiety hamster wheel.

And every time my mind started to drift today, I intentionally refocused.

I've recited and affirmed the truth of God in this verse and all the verses we've learned so far. In doing so, I've wondered if God has used these particularly hard things to help me learn how to live out these verses. I've been more anxious, more pressed, more stressed than normal, which has forced me to continuously redirect my thinking on the true, noble, right, pure, lovely, admirable, excellent, praiseworthy things of God minute by minute. And the peace of Christ has truly guarded my mind and kept me on the right path.

I wonder about you.

How have these verses been the true and lovely things you've been thinking about these past weeks? How have you experienced God's nearness and kindness?

WHAT'S THE POINT?

Write Philippians 4:8. Say it aloud. Take a moment to sit with it before moving forward.

What focus points do you see in this verse?

Here are two I want us to explore together:

- The importance of our thought lives

- What we should think about

We'll use these two questions to guide our study of this verse:

- Why do our thought lives matter?

- How does dwelling on what's virtuous impact our lives?

We'll examine the first question today, then break up the eight listed virtues into two days so we can spend focused time on them. Let's jump in!

LOOK IN THE BOOK

The Focus: The importance of our thought lives

The Question: Why do our thought lives matter?

What does right thinking lead to? Through his testimony in Philippians 3:1-11, Paul stated that to be right with God comes only through faith in Jesus. Righteousness can't be earned; it's given (3:9). This is the central concept of the Bible—the true and right message we all so desperately need. Although we looked at this passage back in Session Three (Phil. 3:1-14; p. 45), I mention it here to give context to the passage we're looking at today. Directly following 3:1-14, this text will show how important right thinking really is.

Read Philippians 3:15–4:1.

> Why did Paul say all mature believers should agree with him ("think this way," CSB) about the gospel message he laid out in Philippians 3:1-14? What if they "think differently" from him?

> Why is what we think about the gospel important?

> How does right thinking inform right living (vv. 15-17)? Where else should we focus our attention if we want to live rightly?

> What did Paul say non-believers set their mind on and what was the ultimate result of this focus (vv. 18-19)?

> What is the ultimate result of a believer's life (vv. 20-21)?

In light of everything Paul said in Philippians 3 about right thinking and right living, he closed with this command in Philippians 4:1, "Therefore . . . stand firm in the Lord in this way."

> How does right thinking and right living lead to standing firm in the Lord?

What have you learned from this passage about the significance of your thought life?

How does your thought life currently impact your behavior? How does it affect your witness and walk with the Lord? What can you start doing or do more faithfully to have a stronger thought life?

Our lives should reflect what we believe about the gospel as we become more and more like Jesus in gospel community. And the ultimate result of our belief is eternity with Him. Hallelujah!

Before we close, I want to consider what doesn't or shouldn't lead us to rejoicing—the state and future of our unbelieving friends. Paul said those apart from Christ have their minds set on earthly things, things which can only fill their bellies for a moment but will never fill their souls. He called them enemies of the cross. That description didn't bring him joy; it brought him to tears.

How does this stark truth about your unbelieving friends hit you? Does it compel you to share your faith with them? Explain.

Paul explained in Philippians 2:5-11 that Jesus humbly stepped down from heaven to be a servant and die for us. And He did so when we were enemies of the cross. Yet, by His grace through faith, He has made us His friends. This is the hope for all of us, including our friends who aren't yet following Christ. It's a hope we can share with them as we reflect the model and mindset of Christ, humbly serving them and loving them sacrificially.

Daily Prayer

O God,

Thank You for all that You teach me in Your Word. Help me to mature my thought life in these ways:

Lord, I confess, I often minimize the significance of having a strong mind focused on You. Help me commit to the practice of refocusing on the good things in Your Word by doing the following:

Lord, I also minimize the significance of what my non-believing friends think about and their standing with You. Please forgive me and burden my heart for them. Please help me share gospel truth with one of them in this way this week:

God, give me a mind that is rooted in Your Word and a heart that is compelled to share Your truth with others.

Amen

True, Noble, Right, and Pure

Fill in the blanks:

Finally, _____ _____ _____, whatever is _____,
whatever is _____, whatever is _____, whatever is _____,
whatever is _____, whatever is _____—if anything is
_____ or _____—think about _____ _____.

Philippians 4:8

___

WE BECOME WHAT WE BEHOLD

Yesterday, we learned that what we think about matters. It shapes our character and informs our actions. What I mean is this:

- Want a life consistent with what you know is true from Scripture and the gospel? Dwell on the truth.

- Want to live a life worthy of respect? Consider what is noble.

- Want a life where you reflect God's righteousness? Meditate on what's right.

- Want a moral life, one unstained by the world? Think about what is pure.

- Want to be known as a lovely person? Think on what's lovely.

- Want to live a life that's well spoken of? Dwell on what's admirable.

- Want to live a life of moral excellence? Think about excellent things.

- Want a life that's worthy of commendation? Focus on praiseworthy things.

This is the goodness and godliness we want our lives to display. What we want our lives to show must first fill our minds. The "how to" is simple: meditate on the goodness found in God's Word. This discipline is what you're learning to do. As we told you from the beginning, memorizing Scripture is the most important part of this study. You are filling your mind and heart with the words of God—true, right, lovely, excellent words—words you can take with you long after this study is in the recycle bin. God's words will go with you, changing how you think and consequently how you live!

Have you seen a change in your life over the last few weeks? Explain.

I have. I've been dwelling on the truth of the nearness of Jesus, and it has changed me. Jesus is near. That simple phrase we memorized back in Session Four has been following me around. In my uncertainty, I have this certainty: "the Lord is near." When I'm worried, I can have peace because "the Lord is near." Every time I feel far off, I fight that feeling with this truth: "the Lord is near." I am more secure, more peaceful, more confident because I am dwelling on this truth.

What about you? Which of the verses we've memorized has impacted your thought life and your actions the most?

LOOK IN THE BOOK

The Focus: What we should think about

The Question: How does dwelling on what's virtuous impact our lives?

Today we're going to look at the first four virtues listed in Philippians 4:8. We're going to consider what the words mean by first defining what they are and what they are not. (Sometimes making that distinction is really helpful for me.) Then, when possible and applicable, we'll look at other places where the words are used in Scripture. We'll also consider how thinking those kinds of thoughts can affect our minds and consequently our lives.

HOW TO DO A WORD STUDY

1. Look up the word in an English dictionary. Read the definition. List the synonyms. Also, note the antonyms to help you consider the opposite meaning.

2. Look up your verse in multiple translations. Our English Bibles were translated from the original languages—Hebrew (Old Testament) and Greek (New Testament). Reading a verse in multiple translations will show you similar but perhaps not the same wording of a passage. This helps you see possible nuances of the words and phrases. An easy way to view multiple translations is to use an app or website like the YouVersion Bible App, biblegateway.com, or biblehub.com.

3. Look up the word in a Bible concordance. While a regular dictionary can be helpful, a concordance will give you the most accurate biblical definition for a word. Concordances also provide references for all the times that word is used in Scripture. This shows you how the Bible uses that word. You can find a free concordance online at biblehub.com. This resource has both *Strong's Exhaustive Concordance* and *Englishman's* Greek and Hebrew concordances.

WHATEVER IS TRUE

What are some synonyms and antonyms for *true*?

Read the following verses to see what the Bible says about truth: Psalm 119:160; John 14:6; John 8:31-32. From these verses, what do you think it means to dwell on truth?

Dwelling on the truth of God's Word always points us to Christ and the ways of Christ. Perhaps there's a reason for truth being first in this list.

How might dwelling on truth more frequently change your thoughts and your actions?

WHATEVER IS NOBLE

How would you define the word *noble*? What's the opposite of noble?

Look up Titus 2:2 and 1 Timothy 3:8,11. The same Greek word used for noble in Philippians 4:8 is found in these verses but not translated as noble.[1] What word or phrase is used instead?

Your translation may say *worthy of respect*, *dignified*, or another synonym. Paul was referring to older men and church leaders in these verses. But from Paul's letter to the Philippians, it's not just a small group in the church who are supposed to be thinking about honorable things and acting with honor. It's all of us.

Do you ever dwell on dishonorable things? How might redirecting your mind to noble things affect your words or your actions?

WHATEVER IS RIGHT

What are some synonyms and antonyms for *right*?

Look up Romans 1:17; 1 Peter 3:18; 1 John 3:7. Write down what they say about righteousness or being right. How do these verses help you understand what it means to dwell on what's right?

The biblical definition of *right* goes beyond our ordinary English definition of merely being correct. It means we are right or righteous before God.

How would focusing on what God sees as right (or righteous) encourage your heart and mind and lead to right actions?

WHATEVER IS PURE

What are some synonyms and antonyms for *pure*? Be sure to look up this one in a concordance (like biblehub.com), as the biblical definition is more specific than our English word.

Look up Philippians 2:14-15 and 1 John 3:3. What do you learn about purity from these verses? How do these verses help you better understand what it means to dwell on what's pure?

The word *pure* in Scripture refers to what God sees as holy, free from sin, morally clean. Keeping our minds in this kind of a pure place amid such an impure world is difficult. Perhaps we should take the same vow as the psalmist in Psalm 101:3: "I will not set before my eyes anything that is worthless. . . . "

What are some impure things you tend to think about? What is one thing you can do to fill your mind with what's pure?

CHALLENGE: Memorize one extra verse this week to help you dwell on what is true, noble, right, or pure. You can choose one of the verses mentioned in this day of study or select a different one from Scripture.

Daily Prayer

Dear God,

You are true. You are noble. You are right. You are pure. You are the perfect expression of all these virtues. Thank You especially that You are:

Father, so often I don't live up to these ways of thinking or living. Please forgive me for how I have fallen short in the following ways:

Lord, sometimes I don't realize how far off my focus is. As I memorize and meditate on this verse, help reorient my thoughts every time I recite it.

Amen

Lovely, Admirable, Excellent, and Praiseworthy

Write out Philippians 4:8.

THE REVERSE OF VIRTUE

Something Jesus said has been following me around.

It's a verse I memorized recently, and it starts off like this: "A good man brings good things out of the good stored up in his heart" (Luke 6:45). Yes! I love and affirm this truth! Anything good that ever comes out of me isn't from me. It's from Jesus! Any true word, any right action, any excellent or praiseworthy thing all comes from Him. Like we mentioned yesterday, when we store up the good things of Christ in our minds and hearts (i.e., all the virtues in our verse), then good things are produced.

But here's the rub: the opposite is also true.

Here's the rest of what Jesus said in Luke 6:45, "and an evil man brings evil things out of the evil stored up in his heart. For the mouth speaks what the heart is full of." While the first part of this verse has followed me around in a positive way reminding me to focus on the virtues in our memory verse, the second half has been hounding me. It reminds me that the bad things that come out of my heart are also the fruit of what I've been storing there.

Ouch!

Case in point: Just this week I've said and done things that are simply not good. This verse tells me those harsh words and wrong actions come from the overflow of my heart. So, when I honestly hold my life up against the list of virtues we've been meditating on, at times I look more like their antonyms.

What we dwell on truly does affect our thoughts and consequently our words and actions, both positively and negatively. The Bible tells us that when we fix our hearts on evil desires, they produce sin in our lives and sin leads to death (Jas. 1:14-15). Too often we believe the lie that we can think evil thoughts or expose ourselves to sinful things and not be corrupted by them, but that is simply not the case. The result of putting evil in our hearts and minds is sin. And sin is dangerous! It separates us from our holy God, interrupts our fellowship with Him, and leads to death—spiritually and sometimes even literally.

So before we study the last four virtues in verse 8, I challenge you to hold your life up against our memory verse and consider whether you look more like the antonyms than the virtues. More than that, consider where you may have become callous or casual about the bad things you're storing up in your heart (either intentionally or unintentionally).

> **Use the space below to confess where you've stored up evil things and ask the Lord to help you give them up and replace them with the virtues in our verse.**

LOOK IN THE BOOK

Today we're going to tackle our last focus point and the related question.

The Focus: What we should think about

The Question: How does dwelling on what's virtuous impact our lives?

We're diving back into Paul's list of things we should think about. We'll discover the meaning of each word and look up other Bible verses containing these words (if applicable) to better understand how dwelling on these virtues might impact our lives.

WHATEVER IS LOVELY

What are some synonyms and antonyms for *lovely*?

This is the only time in the Bible the word *lovely* is used. One scholar translated the phrase "whatever is lovely" as "what calls forth love." It's a word that means pleasing, agreeable, attractive, or winsome. We should think thoughts that result in us being attractive to the world, someone who calls forth admiration, rather than anger or hostility.[2]

How is it possible that what we think about influences our character?

How might thinking lovely or agreeable thoughts translate into winsome character that would reflect God and perhaps lead to a conversation about Jesus?

WHATEVER IS ADMIRABLE

How would you define the word *admirable*? What's the opposite of admirable?

As with *lovely*, this is the only place in the New Testament we find this Greek word.[3] It carries the connotation of thinking thoughts worthy of admiration and not those that would be offensive to God or others.

> How would dwelling on what is admirable affect our walk with the Lord and our witness to the world?

IF ANYTHING IS EXCELLENT

> How would you define the word *excellent*? What is the opposite of excellent?

This was the only time Paul used the word *excellent*. However, in Peter's letters, it's translated as *praise*, *virtue*, or *goodness* (1 Pet. 2:9; 2 Pet. 1:3).[4] It seems to always point the believer toward living a life of moral excellence.

> How does this explanation help you understand what Paul was saying in Philippians 4:8?

> How will dwelling on "the excellencies of God" help us live with moral excellence?

IF ANYTHING IS PRAISEWORTHY

> How would you define the word *praiseworthy*? What is the opposite of praiseworthy?

Look up 1 Peter 1:7. What makes something worthy of praise or commendation?

Peter said it's the proven character of faith that is praiseworthy. And the ability to live out that kind of character starts with the mind, thinking on those things that make God praiseworthy.

How does dwelling on what's praiseworthy help you live a life of commendable character?

Praiseworthy and *excellent* are more generalized words. Why do you think Paul separated them out from the bigger list? How do they work like a catch-all to make his list exhaustive?

In typical Paul fashion, he wasn't leaving anything out. He wanted us thinking on every possible good thing—the lovely, admirable, excellent, praiseworthy things of God displayed in Christ and in His Word.

How might you fill your head with such things today?

Daily Prayer

Dear Lord,

You created this world, and You make good things. I praise You for all that is lovely and admirable and excellent and praiseworthy. Specifically, I think of these things:

But Father, I tend to fill my mind with what's bad and wrong. Forgive me for being lazy or selfish and not doing the good, hard work of focusing on what's good. Forgive me for focusing too much on these negative things:

Lord, help me love the things You love and not be tainted by the world. I realize that what I think about greatly affects how I live. Help me dwell on Your attributes, especially these aspects of Your character:

Amen

Right Thinking, Applied

Write out all the verses you've learned so far. If you need more space, feel free to use the Reflections page!

Ok friend, it's your turn to reflect on and respond to what you've learned this week. Use the following questions as prompts.

- What are the most significant things you learned? What were your "aha moments," if any?

- Where did you feel convicted by this verse?

- What changes do you need to make in your thoughts, attitudes, actions?

- How did your perspective of this verse change through the week as you studied it and meditated on it?

- In what ways do you tend to focus on false, wrong, shameful, disgraceful things? Confess those to God and ask Him to forgive you.

- Which of the virtues listed in verse 8 do you struggle most to dwell on? Why? Write out each of the virtues in Philippians 4:8. Then write how Christ is the fulfillment of each one.

- What are some lovely things you dwell on? What about admirable? Excellent? Praiseworthy?

- How has memorizing this verse impacted your thinking this week? How has it impacted the way you live?

Reflections

Verses

FBAS

WIT
WIN
WIR

WIP
WIL
WIA

IAIEOPTAST
P4.8

WYHLOR
OHFM
SIM
PIIPAT
GOPW
BWY P4.9

R

I
T
L
A
I
W
S
I
A

R

P
4
.
4

I
Yg
bet
at
L
in
p4.
5

D N B A A A B I E S
B P A P W T
PYRTG
P4.6

ATPOG WTAU WGYH AYM ICJ P4.7

Daily Prayer

Write your own prayer today. Thank God for the specific things He's taught you. Confess where you fall short. Ask Him to continue to use this verse to make you more like Jesus!

\
\
\
\
\
\
\
\
\
\
\
\
\
\
\
\
\
\
\
\
\
\
\
\

Viewer Guide

Watch the Session Seven video. Use this page to take notes, capture quotes, or doodle some thoughts from the video teaching session.

Discussion Questions

Discuss the following questions with your Bible study group. A more extensive leader guide is available for free download at **LIFEWAY.COM/DWELL**.

1. What's one thing that stood out to you in this video teaching? Why?

2. If you could create a pie chart showing everything you're thinking about for one whole day, what are the biggest pieces of the pie?

3. Of the eight virtues listed, which one gets too little of your time and which one do you think about the most? Explain.

4. Of the eight virtues listed, which one do you aspire to give more attention to? Why?

5. Why is what we think about so critical to the intimacy of our relationship with Christ and to the effectiveness of our witness for Him?

6. How are you challenged by what you've heard in this video teaching?

7. Why is it so important for you to memorize this verse?

TO ACCESS THE VIDEO TEACHING SESSIONS, USE THE

INSTRUCTIONS IN THE BACK OF YOUR BIBLE STUDY BOOK.

Learn From Me

session eight

Quick Wins!

- Download the Scripture art to your phone, watch, or computer

- Watch the short memory verse video

- Apply the temporary verse tattoo found at the back of your Bible study book

SCRIPTURE ART DOWNLOAD

MEMORY VERSE: PHILIPPIANS 4:9

Or visit **LIFEWAY.COM/DWELL** for all memory verse videos and Scripture art downloads.

WYHLOR OHFM ⊙SIM PIIPAT GOPW BWY P4.9

Set Up for Success

Whatever you have learned or received or heard from me, or seen in me—put it into practice. And the God of peace will be with you. — Philippians 4:9

YOUR FIRST THOUGHTS

Let's take a quick look at our verse for the week. What are your initial thoughts?

What does this verse tell us about God?

What is your initial response to this verse?

What does this verse tell us to do?

Who have you looked to as an example of how you should live? Why that person? Have you had someone look to you in that way? If so, describe that relationship.

Why is it important to have people worthy of imitating in our lives?

MY THOUGHTS

- What if we put into practice everything we've learned in this study?

- What if we rejoiced in the Lord and His salvation all the time?

- What if we were truly gentle with all people?

- What if we lived like Jesus was right here with us?

- What if in every situation we gave our anxieties to God in prayer?

- What if the peace of God was constantly guarding our hearts and minds?

- What if our thought lives were filled with truth, purity, loveliness, and all the other virtues listed?

This kind of living is possible! From what we know of Paul through Acts and his letters, this is the way he lived. You can have a life that looks like his did—one that is sold out to Jesus, that rejoices in every situation, deals with others gently, exchanges worries for peace, has a safe heart and mind, is filled with peace, and is focused on the things of God. And most importantly, as you live like this, "the God of peace will be with you."

I want this kind of life!

I believe you do too.

So, this week we're going to study verse 9 and the promise it contains. Then we're going to look back over what we've learned and analyze our progress in applying all the verses. We'll close the study with a final challenge of how to continue to grow as we live out these truths.

Daily Prayer

Dear Lord Jesus,

Thank You for this passage of Scripture. I've learned so much. Specifically, I'm thankful for learning the following:

But Lord, what good is all this knowledge without life change? Please help me apply what I've learned. Specifically, help me to apply this:

Jesus, help me see where I could establish a better practice of living a life that is pleasing to You. Please give me insight for this specific goal:

Jesus, You are so good. Thank You for working in my life through Your Word!

Amen

Mentoring Matters

Whatever you have learned or received or heard from me, or seen in me—put it into practice. And the God of peace will be with you. — Philippians 4:9

WHO ARE YOU FOLLOWING? WHO'S FOLLOWING YOU?

"You're Natalie who never looks up."

This is how Jo, one of my favorite baristas at the local coffee shop, identified me one morning as I placed my order. I'd been coming there every morning for several months. Unbeknownst to me, that was my nickname behind the counter. When I asked why, Jo told me, "No matter what happens, you never look up." I'd never really thought about it, but she was right. For example, one day a grown man was skateboarding around the center table, and I just kept working, head down, ball cap low. To be honest, that's pretty much my M.O. But apparently, if you don't look up when weird things happen, people notice.

People always notice.

Humans are curious and social creatures. We're constantly looking to see what other people are doing, talking about, wearing, and even eating. I could go on a whole diatribe here, but you get the point. Consider this:

Who are you watching?

Who are you looking to as an example? Do you have a person or (even better) some people you look to when you need to figure out that job thing, or that relationship difficulty, or how to get your kids to wear pants and then later pants that are appropriate? Who's the gentle someone you can call when you're anxious, the one who prays with you and points you to the true, right, pure, lovely things? Who's the someone you not only call on but the one you observe and imitate, the person living out her faith through thick and thin in front of you and with you?

If you have that person in your life, consider going a step further and ask her to mentor you. Basically, she's already doing that, but asking her would formalize it. Schedule regular times to get together for coffee, to chat, pray, and study Scripture together.

We all need these kinds of people, ones who can be an example to us.

Our verse today speaks to this. Paul told the Philippians they should do whatever they had heard and received (think "believed") from him about the gospel and how to walk with Christ. They weren't to follow just what they heard from him but also what they had seen practiced in his life. This is life imitating life. And it's crucial to living out this verse.

We all need to follow after someone who's following Jesus (1 Cor. 11:1). We need examples. We need those we can imitate who are imitating Jesus.

WHAT'S THE POINT?

Write Philippians 4:9. Say it aloud. Take a moment to sit with it before moving forward.

What focus points do you see in this verse?

Here are two for us to explore:

- Following Paul's life and teaching
- The presence of the God of peace

We can use these questions to guide our study this week:

- How do we follow Paul's example so others would want to follow us?
- What does it mean for the God of peace to be with us?

Let's start with the first question.

LOOK IN THE BOOK

The Focus: Following Paul's life and teaching

The Question: How do we follow Paul's example so others would want to follow us?

One thing we need to note is the repetition found in verses 8-9 that we don't see in the English (mainly because the translation would be awkward). Each list ends in the same way:

Paul's list of virtues ends with "these things, think about."

Paul's teaching and lifestyle list ends with "these things, do."

> **How does seeing this repetition help you understand the relationship between right thinking and right living?**

> **In verse 9, what four things did Paul tell the Philippians to put into practice? How does that show Paul's life was consistent with his teaching?**

> **Look up Philippians 1:12-17.** What was Paul going through and how was his example empowering other believers?

> **Think of a person you've seen rely on Jesus through a hard season of life. How were you encouraged by their faith? How were they a role model for you?**

> **Look up Philippians 3:17.** What was Paul's full instruction in this verse?

We aren't physically able to hear Paul's teaching or observe the way he lived his life. But Scripture reveals many of those details, so he remains a model to us. However, in 3:17, Paul also urged the Philippians (and us) to imitate or model our lives after other believers who are walking in biblical faithfulness. In doing so, we must keep in mind that no human is perfect, regardless of the depth of their faith. They will make mistakes. They will sin.

As did Paul. That's why, in 1 Corinthians 11:1, Paul didn't just say "Follow my example." He qualified it, "Follow my example, *as I follow the example of Christ*" (italics mine).

> **Think of people who have positively influenced your life. Why did you look to them for guidance or as a model for how you should live? How has your faith grown stronger because of them?**

> **Are there people who look to you for direction or as someone they can imitate? If so, how do you view that responsibility? If not, what might be the reason?**

> **Someone has said there are two people we should have in our lives: one that is pouring into us and one we are pouring into. How might that be a benefit to our walk with Christ?**

> **Do you have these two people in your life? If not, how might you start pursuing those kinds of relationships?**

We need real life human examples of what living for Christ looks like! Over the years, I've been mentored by a handful of women. They are wise women who are further along in the faith and who've been willing to walk with me through different seasons of my own faith journey. They're not perfect, and I don't expect them to be. But they've met with me, heard me, prayed for me, and have practically shown me how to follow our ultimate model, Jesus. I don't know where I'd be without their willingness to mentor me and be an up-close example of godly living. And I'm so humbled to have been this kind of person for others over the years. I pray I have faithfully and rightly modeled Christ.

Pouring into, being poured into. We all need the example of Christ being modeled for us and being reflected by us as we walk in obedience to Him.

Daily Prayer

Dear Lord,

Thank You for putting godly people in my life. Thank You for their example—for the tangible, practical ways I can see them living out their faith. Thank you especially for:

Lord, remind me that people are looking to me as an example of godly living. Please forgive me for how I've not followed You in these ways:

Thank You for Your Spirit, Lord, who helps me live as I know I should. Help me live more like You specifically in this way:

Lord, please help me be committed to growing in a mentoring relationship in this way:

Thank You, Father, for Your church.

Amen

The God of Peace

Fill in the blanks:

Whatever you have _____ _____ _____ _____
_____ from me, or _____ in me—put it _____ _____.
And the _____ _____ _____ will be with you.

— **Philippians 4:9**

THE GOD OF PEACE

We can have the peace of God.

Paul said pray and it will be given to you. Peace that guards our hearts and minds. Peace we need when we're worried and worn. Peace we experience because Jesus is near. Peace that doesn't make sense in light of the circumstances. Peace that's available for all who are in Christ. Why?

Our God is the God of peace.

He is the ruler and master of it. He conceived and created it. He is the source and maintainer, and He alone owns any and all peace. He is the beginning and the end of peace. And His peace is unbound, transcendent, incomprehensible, profound.

And He wants to give us this peace.

God went to great lengths, spared no expense, and endured shame and sorrow to extend such peace to us. And He was pleased to do so—pleased to send His Son and, "through him to reconcile to himself all things, whether things on earth or things in heaven, by making peace through his blood, shed on the cross" (Col. 1:20). The peace of God was made available to us, not in a peaceful way but a violent one, through the shedding of innocent blood for the guilty. This is the priceless peace that came near in Christ, peace for all time.

LOOK IN THE BOOK

The Focus: The presence of the God of peace

The Question: What does it mean for the God of peace to be with us?

This isn't the first time in this study we've learned about God's peace and presence. Let's refresh our memories.

Review Session Four, Day Three (pp. 70–73) and jot down some truths you learned about the nearness of God.

Review Session Six, Day Two (pp. 115–119) and note some features that stood out to you about the peace of God.

God is near. Through Christ we are brought near to God and experience the peace His salvation brings. Because of His nearness, we can cast our cares on Him (1 Pet. 5:7). We can lay our anxiety and worry at His feet through prayer and experience an unexplainable peace that will guard our hearts and minds.

As Paul finished out this passage and began to close his letter, he referred again to God's peace and presence. He closed many of his letters this way.

Let's look at five of those instances below, including today's verse. Write under each verse what you learn about the peace and the presence of God.

The God of peace will soon crush Satan under your feet. The grace of our Lord Jesus be with you.

ROMANS 16:20

Finally, brothers and sisters, rejoice! Strive for full restoration, encourage one another, be of one mind, live in peace. And the God of love and peace will be with you.

2 CORINTHIANS 13:11

Write out Philippians 4:9.

May God himself, the God of peace, sanctify you through and through. May your whole spirit, soul and body be kept blameless at the coming of our Lord Jesus Christ.

1 THESSALONIANS 5:23

Now may the Lord of peace himself give you peace at all times and in every way. The Lord be with all of you.

2 THESSALONIANS 3:16

Why do you think Paul would regularly want to remind his friends of the powerful working and the constant presence of the God of peace at the end of his letters?

For the Philippians and most early New Testament believers, the world they lived in was not one of peace. Not only did they experience hardships that came with living in a broken world, opposition and persecution would press down on them because of their faith in this God of peace. They would need to be reminded that in their suffering God was close, that He saw them, and that in the end, He would be their victory. Those truths undoubtedly brought peace in the midst of turmoil.

Which of these verses most resonated with you today? Why?

One last thing to notice about verse 9 is that we most intimately experience God's fellowship when we obey Him. Of course, God is always with us in relationship. But if we choose to live in sinful disobedience, our fellowship with Him is interrupted. Only as we continually put into practice the truth of Scripture will we fully experience His presence. As one scholar put it, "God's peace especially resides in those who have ordered their lives in accordance with God's will."[1]

Daily Prayer

God of peace,

Thank You for all I've learned about Your peace and presence today. I'm specifically grateful for this truth:

Lord, I confess I don't always live like You are the God of peace. I seek my peace in flimsy, temporal things. Please forgive me for looking to the following things to give me peace:

Lord, help me live in faithful obedience to You so I can enjoy close fellowship with You. Give me strength to obey You in the following ways:

Thank You for Christ who has given me this costly peace I could never earn.

Amen

WYHLOR
OHFM
◉SIM
PIIPAT
GOPW
BWY P4.9

Whatever You Have Seen

Write out Philippians 4:9.

LIVE THIS WAY

I love when my son, Josiah, calls from college.

But I hate saying goodbye. I know he's out in the world now, making all his own decisions (seems like mostly good ones), but I'm not there with him like I once was. I'm not part of his life day-in and day-out. I love my son, and want him to thrive. But I can't advise him in every situation or give him wisdom for every decision. Some I can speak into, but most are now handled apart from me. So, whenever we chat and it's time to say goodbye, I tell him I love him, miss him, and am proud of him. Then, once we're off the phone I pray for him. I pray that all the good things he's learned from his dad and me will take root in him and impact his choices, his words, and his actions.

In Philippians 4:4-9, Paul was starting to say goodbye.

He was coming to the end of his conversation with his long-distance friends—friends he held dear and wanted to see thrive. But he couldn't be there with them, advising every situation, giving wisdom for every decision. So, he pointed them to his example. They were to remember how he'd lived and what he'd taught them and live in such a way. Paul was being practical, not conceited. He wasn't trying to take the place of Christ in their lives, just pointing them toward Him through his witness. As we said yesterday, we all need someone who's walking with Jesus to help show us the way of Jesus. We need someone to model godliness and help us apply biblical principles in our lives. Hopefully, in some small way, you've found that in this study.

And like Paul, it's time for us to say goodbye.

I hope you've loved our time together as much as I have. As we close, my prayer for you is that you would live out what you've learned and received and heard and seen in this study. Remember, I told you early in the study that if I could give you one thing I would give you God's Word. Well, I hope you've gotten it—not just in your head, but deep in your heart, and that you'll live it out more and more in your daily life. I hope the verses you've memorized have been and will be the words on your mind in the middle of the night, the words you pray back to God, the words that come out of your mouth when you're talking with friends, the words that correct you and inspire your right living. I hope you've been changed by the practice of memorizing and meditating on God's Word.

Please don't say goodbye to the practice of Scripture memory!

I urge you to commit to memorize more and more of God's Word. Whenever you're reading or studying your Bible and you find a verse that stands out to you: memorize it! Here's a quick tip to help: Keep three-by-five inch note cards in or near your Bible. When you find a verse or passage you want to memorize, write out the first letter of every word on one side of the card, and write the verse or passage on the back. Put that card somewhere you will see it often and quiz yourself until you've got it down.

This practice is what Vera and I do.

And it's what we help other people do too. Every single month, we memorize and meditate on one Bible verse with a whole community of people. And we'd love for you to join us! Just come on over to dwelldifferently.com to check out our weekly podcast, devotionals, and social posts. We'd love the privilege of continuing to help you connect with God through the simple practice of dwelling on His Word.

What's been the most impactful part of memorizing this passage of Scripture?

VERSE REVIEW

To close, let's revisit each verse. Next to each design, write the verse. Then, write what God taught you through the verse. Finally, write a prayer for how you would like to continue to apply this verse in your life. (This exercise is in lieu of our daily prayer for today.)

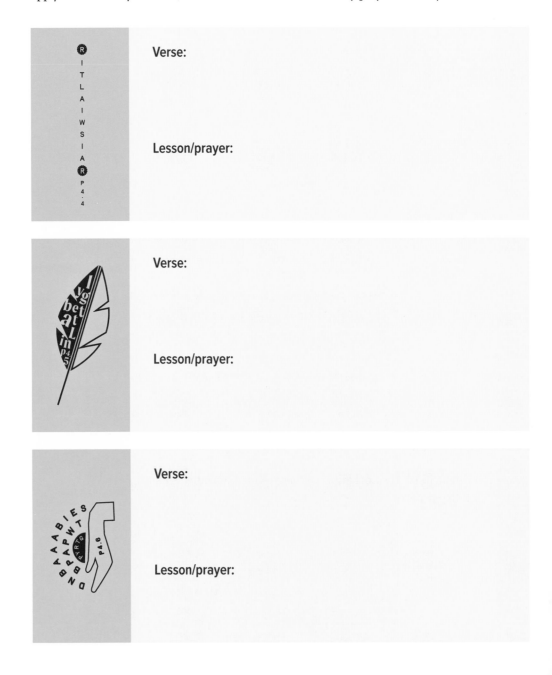

Verse:

Lesson/prayer:

Verse:

Lesson/prayer:

Verse:

Lesson/prayer:

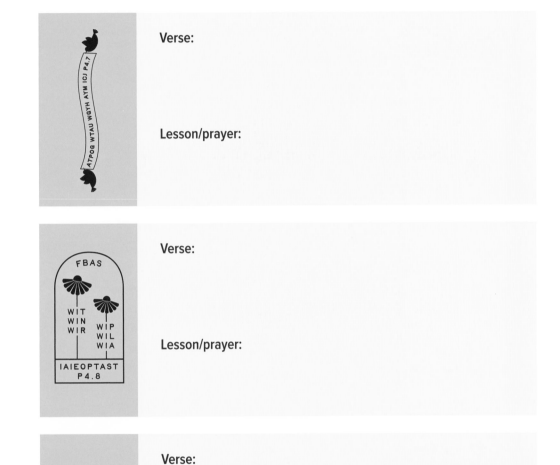

Verse:

Lesson/prayer:

Verse:

Lesson/prayer:

Verse:

Lesson/prayer:

Final Application

JOURNALING PROMPTS

For this week:

- What are the most significant things you learned from the study of Philippians 4:9? What were your "aha" moments, if any?

- Where did you feel convicted by this verse?

- What changes do you need to make in your thoughts, attitudes, actions?

- How does this verse encourage us to live out what we've learned in this study?

- Do you have a mentor? Is someone pouring into you? Are you pouring into someone else? If not, what steps are you taking to include these people in your life?

- Are you currently living a life for Christ that is worth imitating? Remember, we're not talking about a perfect life but one of growing, devoted, faithfulness to the Lord. If not, what needs to change?

For this study:

- Where did you see transformation in your mind, heart, or actions through the course of this Bible study?

- How did you grow in your understanding of God?

- What did you learn about yourself?

- What is your biggest takeaway from this study? What was the most significant thing you learned?

- How did this study impact the way you think about Scripture memory?

- Are you committed to continuing memorizing Scripture? Why or why not? If so, what is one verse you want to memorize going forward?

Reflections

Reflections

Dwell on These Things

Daily Prayer

Write your own prayer today. Thank God for the specific things He's taught you. Confess where you fall short. Ask Him to continue to use this verse to make you more like Jesus!

Viewer Guide

Watch the Session Eight video. Use this page to take notes, capture quotes, or doodle some thoughts from the video teaching session.

Discussion Questions

Discuss the following questions with your Bible study group. A more extensive leader guide is available for free download at **LIFEWAY.COM/DWELL**.

1. What's one thing that stood out to you in this video teaching? Why?

2. Who's someone who has been influential in your spiritual growth? In what ways?

3. Why do you think it's important to have someone you pour into and someone pouring into you?

4. If you're currently mentoring someone, share about that experience (without revealing names or anything confidential).

5. Are you living the kind of life where you could honestly and sincerely say, "Whatever you have learned or received or heard from me, or seen in me—put it into practice"? Explain.

6. How are you challenged by what you've heard in this video teaching?

7. Why is it so important for you to memorize this verse?

TO ACCESS THE VIDEO TEACHING SESSIONS, USE THE

INSTRUCTIONS IN THE BACK OF YOUR BIBLE STUDY BOOK.

How to Become a Christian

Romans 10:17 says, "Faith comes from hearing the message, and the message is heard through the word about Christ."

Maybe you've stumbled across new information in this study. Or maybe you've attended church all your life, but something you read here struck you differently than it ever has before. If you have never accepted Christ but would like to, read on to discover how you can become a Christian.

Your heart tends to run from God and rebel against Him. The Bible calls this sin. Romans 3:23 says, "For all have sinned and fall short of the glory of God"

Yet God loves you and wants to save you from sin, to offer you a new life of hope. Jesus says in John 10:10b, "I have come that they may have life, and have it to the full."

To give you this gift of salvation, God made a way through His Son, Jesus Christ. Romans 5:8 says, "But God demonstrates his own love for us in this: While we were still sinners, Christ died for us."

You receive this gift by faith alone. Ephesians 2:8-9 says, "For it is by grace you have been saved, through faith—and this is not from yourselves, it is the gift of God—not by works, so that no one can boast."

Faith is a decision of your heart demonstrated by the actions of your life. Romans 10:9 says, "If you declare with your mouth, 'Jesus is Lord,' and believe in your heart that God raised him from the dead, you will be saved."

If you trust that Jesus died for your sins and want to receive new life through Him, pray a prayer similar to the following to express your repentance and faith in Him:

Dear God, I know I am a sinner. I believe Jesus died to forgive me of my sins. I accept Your offer of eternal life. Thank You for forgiving me of all my sins. Thank You for my new life. From this day forward, I will choose to follow You.

If you have trusted Jesus for salvation, please share your decision with your group leader or another Christian friend. If you are not already attending church, find one in which you can worship and grow in your faith. Following Christ's example, ask to be baptized as a public expression of your faith.

Endnotes

SESSION TWO

1. T. Robertson, *Word Pictures in the New Testament* (Nashville, TN: Broadman Press, 1933), Php 4:8.

SESSION FIVE

1. Strong's G3309: merimnaō, Blue Letter Bible, https://www.blueletterbible.org/lexicon/g3309/niv/mgnt/0-1/.

SESSION SIX

1. Strong's G5432: phroureō, Blue Letter Bible, https://www.blueletterbible.org/lexicon/g5432/niv/mgnt/0-1/.

2. John F. MacArthur Jr., *Philippians, MacArthur New Testament Commentary* (Chicago: Moody Press, 2001), 285.

3. Strong's G3956: pas, Blue Letter Bible, https://www.blueletterbible.org/lexicon/g3956/niv/mgnt/0-1/.

4. Strong's G1097: ginōskō, Blue Letter Bible, https://www.blueletterbible.org/lexicon/g1097/esv/mgnt/0-1/.
   Strong's G1107: gnōrizō, Blue Letter Bible, https://www.blueletterbible.org/lexicon/g1107/kjv/tr/0-1/.

SESSION SEVEN

1. Strong's G4586: semnos, Blue Letter Bible, https://www.blueletterbible.org/lexicon/g4586/niv/mgnt/0-1/.

2. Gerald F. Hawthorne, *Philippians, vol. 43, Word Biblical Commentary* (Dallas: Word, Incorporated, 2004), 251.

3. Ibid.

4. Richard R. Melick, *Philippians, Colossians, Philemon, vol. 32, The New American Commentary* (Nashville: Broadman & Holman Publishers, 1991), 151.

SESSION EIGHT

1. Richard R. Melick, *Philippians, Colossians, Philemon, vol. 32, The New American Commentary* (Nashville: Broadman & Holman Publishers, 1991), 151.

Notes

Looking for more?

Check out these studies we think you'll love!

The Bible in a Year
By Kandi Gallaty

In this one-year journey from Genesis through Revelation, walk through key passages of the Bible at a manageable, five-days-per-week pace.

Encountering God
By Kelly Minter

Unpack the biblical foundation for certain sacred habits along with approachable ways to practice disciplines like prayer, study, worship, rest, and many more.
(7 sessions)

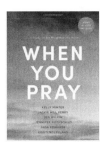

When You Pray
By Kelly Minter, Jackie Hill Perry, Jen Wilkin, Jennifer Rothschild, Jada Edwards, and Kristi McLelland

Study six prayers in the Bible that can renew and inspire your own.
(7 sessions)

TruthFilled
By Ruth Chou Simons

Study the book of Colossians as you learn the practice of preaching gospel truth to yourself by studying Paul's example.
(7 sessions)

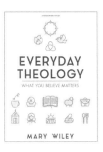

Everyday Theology
By Mary Wiley

Explore 8 essential doctrines: Scripture, God, Jesus, the Holy Spirit, humanity, salvation, the church, and the end times to get to know God more deeply.
(8 sessions)

From Beginning to Forever
By Elizabeth Woodson

See how all 66 books of the Bible combine to form one unified narrative.
(7 sessions)

lifeway.com/women | 800.458.2772

Pricing and availability subject to change without notice.

Lifeway women

Get the most from your study.

Customize your Bible study time with a guided experience.

In this study you'll:

- Discover how dwelling on Scripture transforms how we think, see, and interact with the world

- Learn a simple method of memorizing Scripture that will equip you to make it a lifelong practice.

- Take a slow walk through Philippians 4:4-9 to fix the truths of this passage in your heart and mind.

- Experience the peace and presence of God as you practice Scripture memorization

STUDYING ON YOUR OWN?

Watch Natalie Abbott and Vera Schmitz's teaching sessions and memory verse videos, available via redemption code for individual video-streaming access, printed in this Bible study book.

LEADING A GROUP?

Each group member will need a *Dwell on These Things* Bible study book, which includes video access. Because all participants will have access to the video content, you can choose to watch the videos outside of your group meeting if desired. Or, if you're watching together and someone misses a group meeting, they'll have the flexibility to catch up! A DVD set is also available to purchase separately if desired.

Browse study formats, a free session sample, video clips, church promotional materials, and more at

lifeway.com/dwell